Menopause

vs.

Puberty

TOMMALISA LUMPKIN

First Electronic Edition, June 2018

First Paperback Edition, June 2019

Copyright © 2019 Tommalisa Lumpkin

www.menopausevspuberty.com

ISBN: 978-1081880576

CONTENTS

	Acknowledgments	vii
	Preface	ix
1	The Challenge	1
2	The Teen Brain	13
3	The Balance	27
4	The Truth	37
5	The Job	49
6	The Divorce	61
7	Harnessing Their Superpowers	75
8	Dig Deep	97
9	The "B" Word	115
10	The Hormones	135
11	T'Lisa-isms	149
12	Epilogue (Parting Thoughts)	165

ACKNOWLEDGMENTS

I dedicate this book to my daughter, Kelsie Kamali Mifflin, and my two sons, TiJuan Maurice Lumpkin Jr., and Thomas Alexander Lumpkin. Watching the three of you grow into young adults has been rewarding. I have never known a love so pure until I met the three of you. Thank you for the years of laughter and learning. I am a better person for having met you and a better mom for having the privilege of raising you. I love you so very much, and may God bless you all the days of your lives.

Thank you to my parents for always loving me through this life unconditionally. Thank you, LaTonya, for always being the world's greatest auntie and sister. To my husband, TiJuan, I am a better mom and wife because of you. None of this would be possible without your love and support. Thank you, babe. I love you so much.

"….and I spent my days, pouring my life without measure…"

~CeCe Winans

MENOPAUSE VS. PUBERTY

PREFACE

This book is a passion project to share my nuggets of wit and wisdom to help women win! I want to encourage moms - especially older moms – and let them know that *they can win at parenting at any age*. I love motivating people and speaking my truths, so I wrote this book to educate, motivate, and inspire older moms to fight back against Mother Nature and use their wisdom to win at parenthood and life. Also, I share my challenges and mistakes to help younger moms avoid the pitfalls that try to trap us. Menopause, in my opinion, is absolutely the best time to be a parent because you're older, wiser, and stronger than those tiny people we call our children! You can outsmart them, and you can win!

No young girl ever dreams of being the mother of pubescent children during her menopausal years. In fact, no young girl dreams of her menopausal years at all. She dreams of white picket fences, knights in shining armor, two kids, and a tiny dog. My dreams were no different growing up. I did not plan to be the mom of young kids at 54. Two marriages, three kids, and one grandson later, I see life from a different vantage point. Life is not at all what I expected it to be, but it is more satisfying than I could have ever imagined. Life experience is a blessing and being an "older mom" is a joy! There are days when hot flashes and mood swings get the best of me, but what I know now about parenting and raising children has changed the game! It was my mom who painted the visual for me one day during our daily chat. She said, "Lisa, certainly you realize that you have the benefit of 10 years of experience over your boys' friends' parents." It was a revelation. I hadn't thought of it in that way, and it was true. I was finally "old" with *really* young kids. The "wise" part was questionable.

I remember when the fear and trepidation of raising two little boys started creeping in. I was in my mid-40's when a panic rushed over me. I'd tell my mom that I was too old to successfully raise these two boys without losing my mind. My mounting fears calmed when I realized what my mom was trying to tell me. She was saying that I was in the advanced class of parenting based on the extra years of experience at life that I'd had from raising my daughter, Kelsie. I had unknowingly prepared for the "master's course" of parenting.

Like many women, I had vowed not to have any more kids after my first one was older than a certain age – actually, I had vowed not to have any more kids at all. However, I met a handsome young man (who was 11 years younger than me), fell in love, and free-fell right into a whole new do-over at life which I didn't plan at all. Sometimes I feel like I'm watching my life through a stranger's eyes! We are raising two amazing young men, and I love my life, but I fight through **zero tolerance** (the lack of patience to fight through puberty's smart-mouth comments and attitudes) daily. I have low patience and the occasional bad attitude myself when met with defiance. Zero tolerance is killing me because when you are a parent, you are forced to be tolerant - and herein lies my struggle. I'm in a boxing match with Mother Nature, and she is whipping my *ss! My "bob and weave" leaves a great deal to be desired, but I'm not giving up without a fight!

When you read this, you will learn that I am *a driven person*. I tend to push myself and my boys to compensate for my fear of failure. I am very impatient with excuses and entitlement, and I don't understand why so many individuals feel as though people owe them something. I refuse to raise these young men to live life beneath their purpose and ability. You must *dig deep* to achieve your dreams - push harder, do more, and outclass the competition. I know those aren't popular sentiments these days but we working women and moms need grit to make it - *and so do our kids*. Working, parenting, and doing life is hard - and there's no way around that.

And don't even get me started on marriage. I've been married twice - I got married to and divorced from my first husband at a young age. I'm not proud of it; it's just a fact. The word "divorce" alone represents ill will and negativity. I have learned a lot about the power of being humble and genuinely giving of yourself, making sacrifices, and giving in to your husband's point of view - *sometimes.* There are times when *I think that I am right* - many times in fact - and am glad I followed my intuition. Other times…. let's just say thank God for the wisdom of my husband and the power of holding your tongue. Seriously, I have found my husband to be wiser and more patient than I could ever have imagined, and he is the perfect balance to my fiery, "take-no-prisoners" approach to life!

I don't have it all figured out, but I've learned a lot on my journey through trial, error, threats, tears, prayer, love, and lots of laughter. Parenting isn't hard – good parenting is hard – and will stretch you in ways you could never have imagined possible. I pray that you will laugh, learn, and be inspired when you read MVP and that you will be encouraged that you are the right woman for the job. Make up your mind that YOU WILL WIN because failure is not an option!

TOMMALISA LUMPKIN

1.

THE CHALLENGE

January 7, 2018

Me: "TJ, where are your basketball clothes? They need to be washed."

TJ: "Uuh uuh uuuuuuuuh, I need to uuh uuh check uuuuh....."

Me: "What are you saying? My God (in the most dramatic way possible), is that your best attempt at communicating with me?" Then, in my head, "Not 👊to- 👊damn- 👊day 👊puberty! What the hell are you saying? Why am I ear hustling? I'm not the problem here…I don't speak this language…Jesus, please give me the strength to not pinch his lips together…I still don't know what he was trying to say to me! It's like puberty gave up on the English language…I don't have the patience for this! Damn clothes could have been in the dryer by now! 😠"

Jan 9, 2017

TJ: "I know what I want to do for my birthday this year."

Me (In my head): "Can't we just get through Lex's birthday this month? Didn't we just have a birthday party for you? Dang, these kids hate me!"

TJ continues to talk over my conversation in my head: "I want to go salmon fishing in Alaska during breeding season. We can catch female salmon and get their caviar…or catch sturgeon for some caviar."

Me (In my head again): "What in the entire hell? Does he know how much it costs to take a family of four to Alaska? Lawd, how have I forsaken thee? What is my child researching? If I'm really still maybe he won't even see me. What the hell is a sturgeon? How do you answer a question like that from a 75-year-old who is supposed to be 13?"

~~~

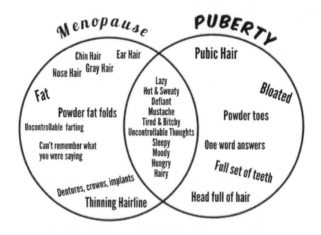

Menopause and puberty can coexist but think long and hard when that handsome young stud of a man asks you to marry him in your late "whatever-age-over-30s!" When my husband proposed to me, every *single* thing about him intoxicated me. His eyes have the sweetest curves to them, and they seem to smile at me every time I look into them, when he speaks on a subject he's 99.9% right about it because he's just brilliant that way (honestly he's quiet and only engages in topics that he' sure he knows something about), and those lips of his are absolutely irresistible. He's extremely intelligent and is the world's greatest father. TiJuan Lumpkin, Sr. is totally committed to building outstanding, educated, and God-fearing young men. I was drawn to Mr. Lumpkin like a magnet, and despite my vows several years prior to never get married again nor have any more babies, I jumped in headfirst. I agreed to have two children when we got married, "and then I'm closing down the shop," is what I told T. The first eight years with the boys were seamless. They grew fast, and for the most part, TJ and Lex were relatively easy children to raise.

It was not until my late 40's to early 50's that I noticed something concerning, and it wasn't the boys - it was my physical and mental ability to handle them. Having given birth to the boys at age 40 and 41, I was already on the path to menopause the day they were born! By the time I'd reached age 54, I had become painfully aware that I was struggling to keep my emotions intact and had been for several years. To add to this emotional state, I would sweat profusely at any given moment and it was particularly embarrassing as it would happen at the worst times in the middle of a conversation with one of my doctors (I'm a Pharmaceutical Sales Representative), during a sales call, or at the checkout counter at the grocery store. I could, on occasion, feel the sweat bead up on my forehead while a rush of sweat was rolling down my back. It was maddening! I also noticed that the slightest monotonous noise drove me insane. Oh, and can I just say that there was noise constantly at any given time with these boys. Whenever TJ and Lex would beatbox, hum, yell, run, dribble the basketball, or even breathe it seemed, I'd have to remove myself from the area. The worst was in small, confined spaces like the car. I became extremely sad and cried frequently about anything, and it became particularly hard to pull myself out of bed for anything other than work. I'd find any excuse I could to turn down outings with friends, and I would always sit in the car **and wait** no matter where or how long it took for the boys to get out of practice. I did this because it became harder and harder to face people.

Many different emotions would sweep over me at the same time, and it would happen randomly and without notice. I felt on edge and had no control over the things I'd say to people. I started having debilitating headaches and extreme panic attacks that I could not explain nor identify their origin. The panic attacks were frightening, and I'm still learning how to calm myself while working through them. I slept four to five hours at most each night, which would make me tired and cranky the following day. I was often short-tempered, irritable, and out of control. Hell, I didn't even want to be around myself, and existing at the whim of my own thoughts was exasperating. I felt as if I was losing control and did not recognize myself. It was then that I realized the life I was currently living wasn't designed with menopause in mind. I pushed and dragged myself through it every day because I had two young happy, vibrant, lively, and eager-to-take-the-world-by storm boys who needed a present mom. Chasing their dreams didn't factor in my 54-year-old

knees and, despite the awesome things the boys were accomplishing, my back was saying, "to hell with it all, I'm out!"

What I didn't know and what I hope to convey to you is that the challenge of having teenagers while you are in the storm of menopause is a monumental hurdle. It will test every fiber of your being! Puberty showed up one day without warning and kicked in my front door. I think I heard one of them say, "We're here, bitches, and our main mission in life is to make you as miserable as possible!"

The pre-pubescent one said, "Yeah, and we're here for the next seven years!" Then, like an army of hungry ants rampaging through the forest, these two bundles of hormones swarmed our kitchen eating everything in sight.

Be ready sisters, because mother nature will kick in and constantly remind you of all the reasons menopause and puberty should never cohabitate. There is no way to know how hard menopause will hit you or to truly understand that when intermingled with the growing pains of puberty, it will make life an absolute hormonal mess. You will cry many tears in the shower, experience many emotions all at the same time several times a day, question your sanity and feel guilty for wanting to pack up all your earthly belongings and drive to the other end of the country in the dead of night undetected. You may even consider purchasing a tiny house just for you built alongside a tiny lake far away in a tiny town no one has ever heard of just to find peace from the "overstimulated" world of puberty. Yeah, you are right, I've given this quite a bit of thought.

It is a wise parent who preps themselves for the inevitable. Teens are wired to push you towards the edge of the precipice without fail. I cannot tell you the number of times I've just stared at my boys while in the middle of an internal emotional meltdown. I have not quite figured out how or why they do the things they do, but I'm convinced that it's a conspiracy. I think they hate me and are systematically plotting my demise. I've also had to curtail the thoughts that run through my mind during episodes of "The Lumpkin Boy" shenanigans. "Lawd Jesus, I'm too old for this $%&!" or "I wonder how much time I'd serve for smacking him across the back of his head?" Alas, saner thoughts prevail, and I resort to the mannequin-style of discipline. Ignore, ignore, ignore. "Maybe they won't even see me if I remain motionless." I'm constantly coaching myself internally. "Listen, don't respond with that thought, you could scar him for life...Girl, just stare at his forehead until he becomes so uncomfortable that he gives in...and my all-time favorite, sarcasm...Did he just mumble a whole sentence to me with the expectation of a response? Hell, I don't even know what he just said." Yeah, I know what you're thinking and yes, staring at foreheads saves lives.

Being the type of parent a pubescent kid needs will require a menopausal parent to push way past the mental and physical pain of what is happening to their own minds and bodies to give puberty what it needs. So, try your best not to fall and break a hip navigating the bleachers to get a good seat to watch their games while you are sitting outside sweating buckets in the heat. Lord knows I'm way too old to have these knees and lower back sitting outside in the middle of winter watching a football game. Yes, my life as an older mom also requires that I do things that my body has emphatically decided not to do. Either way, I do it anyway because I love my kids, and it's important to support them.

Puberty has taken me by surprise. While I should be teaching my boys how to have politically correct conversations, I tend to give it to them raw and unabridged. It's becoming harder and harder to protect them and their ears from my knee jerk reactions and the "hit them between the eyes with reality" responses. I imagine the 25 or 30-year-old moms gently saying, "Honey, get the bleach and a pair of gloves and clean up your mess in the bathroom." My typical response can be heard across all three levels of our home in a loud, angry yelling manner, "I DON'T CARE WHO PISSED ON THE BATHROOM FLOOR BUT Y'ALL GOT EXACTLY TWO MINUTES TO CLEAN IT UP BEFORE I COME UP IN THIS PIECE TAKING BRUTHAS OUT!!!!!" I am absolutely exhausted by the male dysfunction with which I must live.

I'm also purposefully tough on my boys because I want them to understand how to be prepared for the random situations life throws their way. Mostly I feel guilty that I've done them a disservice by choosing to be a mom so late in life. I find myself wanting to give them a crash course on life should I die while they are still young! The consequence of it makes me sad. When I was 35 and 40, I felt like I had all the time in the world to live. Now, in my mid 50's, the thought of never seeing either of the boys have kids or watching them grow to be old men haunts me. There are pros and cons to every decision we make in life, and this one, in particular, exposes my lack of thinking through what having babies in my 40's really means. It also makes me push harder at healthier living so that I can stretch my years as far out as possible. I want to be around if they should ever need me in the way that my parents are here for me now. However, the sad reality is that when the boys are in their late forties, I'll be in my late eighties. Gasp!

Despite my efforts to be strong and bold in the face of my husband and two young boys, I am sometimes stricken with sheer terror at the thought of their pain when I die. Death is hard enough when it happens organically at the average age parents pass away. I secretly feel guilty that I made a selfish decision by not considering the full implications of what having children later in life means. I've even romanticized narrating my funeral by recording a comedic eulogy along with a video to make my kids laugh so that they won't focus on being sad. I imagine them walking through the funniest moments of our lives together and reminding them to strive for greatness in all that they desire to achieve in life.

Even when these thoughts creep in and move me to tears, I'm still rejoicing in God's favor. I would do it all over again if I had the chance because my kids are absolutely awesome and amazing, and I can't imagine this world missing out on the opportunity of meeting them. They are the reason my heart skips a beat every single day. When you add my little grandbaby in with my three greatest works (Kelsie, TiJuan Jr., and Lex), I'd be selfish for **NOT** having them. So yes, I'm glad I had more kids, and I pray they understand when the time comes. If you've had these thoughts, I hope you feel the same way. Parenting at any age is such a blessing; it is worth it no matter what comes!

On the flip side, the boys get the advantage of my wisdom from a whole different perspective of experiences. I'm more mellow and laid back than I used to be as a younger mom with Kelsie. I've also learned that my boys will meet and match the mood I give them. I still give too many instructions at once, and that is one of the parent-fails that I am working to control. I'm also more committed to showing my kids "tough love," and I don't apologize for it. If one of the boys leaves their bookbag at home, I'm not going to go out of my way to get it to them. One of the boys forgot his basketball shoes at home and called to ask me to bring them to him for practice. I told him that I'd be an awful mom if I did and that he would have to figure it out. He has never forgotten his shoes again. Lol! He borrowed a pair from one of his teammates.

I certainly did not look ahead long enough to see the puberty years coming when the boys were little. I knew that they were inevitable and the last time I'd seen puberty I was not going through menopause. Puberty and menopause are the synonyms of hormones. They are two contrasting ideas, but they have the same effect. You don't go skydiving, cliff-hanging, BASE jumping, or bull riding without the proper training and equipment, do you? When you invite puberty to live in a menopausal environment, you must be ready for anything. You must do your research to gain an understanding of where you and your teen are heading. Winging it won't cut it. There are too many rapid changes, unpredictable and explosive moments lurking around the corner. When you couple that with drugs, vaping, sex, teenage pregnancy, STD's, social media, suicide, and all the dangerous "challenges" (The Blue Whale, The Kylie Jenner Lip, The Fire, The Banana Sprite, The Eraser, The 72-hour, and many others) out there, you have the makings for a disaster. There is also the pesky fact that some menopausal moms have yet to learn how to decode teen text abbreviations or slang.

To help me learn more, a good friend, HH, told me about a new book, *The Teenage Brain*. I'm a geek when it comes to the human brain and hearing that a neurologist had written a book on the adolescent brain was so exciting. I couldn't wait to pick it up! As I turned the pages, everything began to make sense.

MENOPAUSE VS. PUBERTY

2.

The Teen Brain

November 15, 2017

This morning while driving Lex to school we heard an interesting news announcement about the singer, Jill Scott's, divorce.

Radio personality: "...I mean I don't know how anyone could divorce Jill Scott. She's a full-figured and beautiful woman with a lovely voice! The woman is a full package, AND she drops hit albums! Man!"

Lex: "What's an album?"

Me: "Well, back in the day... (First thought to myself: You know you're old when you start a sentence with "back in the day! 😫") ...long before CDs and downloads were a thing, we had to use a record player to play records. Records were round, and you could play a single song or a whole album with many songs. (Second thought to myself: Did I just say "record player?" Damn, I'm old!)

Lex: "What's a record player? (Third thought to myself: Really Lex! Are we doing THIS this morning, huh?!") Do we have one?"

Me: "We don't, and here is a picture of one."

Lex: "That looks really old! Wow, how long ago was this? I knew you were old, but I didn't know you were THAT old! Wow!"

~~~

Dr. Effie Maude Shannon-Alexander has been a champion of teens and families for as long as I have known her. Her ongoing work in the community spans decades. If she recognized an unmet need, she'd organize, coordinate, and/or became founder or co-founder of whatever could be the potential solution. She has served each level in public education: Classroom Teacher, Guidance Counselor (K-Adult), Assistant Principal, Dean, Information Services Specialist, District Administrator, and Director of Safe Schools and Community Services at the Florida State Department of Education in Tallahassee. Dr. Shannon-Alexander holds numerous professional degrees and certifications including a B.S. in Elementary Education, M.S. Degrees in Guidance Counseling, Supervision, and Administration (K-Adult), a MS +15 in Children and Families,

Information Services, and Vocational Education, and a Ph.D. in Human Services and Spiritual Counseling. You can only imagine what the rest of her resume is like - and to top it all off, *she's my mom!*

In addition to raising my sister and me, my mother spent well over 42 years (1963 through 2005) dedicated to improving future outcomes for the teens and young adults of Pinellas County and the State of Florida. I share this condensed version of my mother's resume not only to lend credence to her knowledge of teenagers but also because I'm so very proud of her and her accomplishments. For most of my younger years, my sister, LaTonya, and I could count 60 or more self-proclaimed "siblings" who claimed our mom as their own as well. She is the "Teen Whisperer."

Our home phone would ring non-stop with teens, and even now, with parents of teens, in search of conversation with her because of her unique way of listening and hearing beyond what's being shared verbally. Somehow mom could speak their language and help them understand and navigate the difficulties of adolescent life. Even on stage in a keynote speech, she seemed to "speak life" into them. I can still remember days when young people would swarm around my mom after a presentation. She has always believed in their ability to achieve and excel. Thus, mom lived in the trenches helping teenagers find jobs, teaching them how to prepare for college entrance exams, and continuously developing community programs that would help them achieve success.

It's clear why I am the way that I am with my teens - I had GREAT examples to follow. My mom and dad were never my "friends" during my teenage years but never made me feel like my thoughts and opinions didn't matter. They both were present in all aspects of my life - both the happy and trying times. I grew up feeling loved and safe. I could be a whole individual without conditions.

Dad was the funniest parent and mom was the most strict. Together they provided a balanced life that built a solid foundation beneath my feet. Dad taught me to be strong in life - to stand tall unapologetically and to make sure that whatever I set out to accomplish that I did it to the very best of my ability. Dad would always say, "no one will ever GIVE you anything in this life. You have to get it yourself." He then set out to prove it to me in various ways. I remember at a very young age my dad would challenge me to race him. He beat me every single time. I remember thinking, "Wow, I thought dad loved me. If he does, then why does he beat me in challenges so miserably every time?" I think he enjoyed beating me. The day I left my dad in a cloud of smoke will be forever imprinted on my mind. I not only beat him hands down in a foot race, but I realized just how much he loved me that day because I realized that there was nothing in the world that I could not accomplish if I worked hard enough to achieve it. I beat dad fair and square, and I did it on my own. What a powerful message to embed on a teenage brain! My parents are amazing people. Little did I know that their parenting strategies were supported by research-based best practices for parenting.

My interest in neuroscience stems from both growing up with a mom who was hyper-focused on creating exceptional outcomes for kids and my 23 years of work in the pharmaceutical industry. I sold three medications for major depression, two for bipolar disorder, one injectable for bipolar disorder, and two long-acting injectables for schizophrenia. I have spent at least 85% of my career on in-patient and crisis intervention units, prisons, Veterans Administration Hospitals, state hospitals, group homes, and other outpatient facilities such as community mental health centers. Primarily, my job was to share the benefits of the medications I sold with psychiatrists, nurse practitioners, injection nurses, assertive community treatment team members, social workers, and pharmacists for their clients who suffered from mental illness. One of the things that always fascinated me was how dedicated they were to helping their clients achieve normalcy, which was often quite challenging. Mental illness can tear even the strongest families apart. When one family member has a diagnosis, everyone is impacted, and trauma can spark a wildfire of trouble in a developing mind where mental illness never existed before. Families often don't consider this when dealing with their teens. Just one traumatic event can shift their thinking in significant ways for a lifetime.

Even when healthy, a "teen brain" is not fully developed and is susceptible to unpredictable disruptions in its thought patterns. You can just imagine what trauma and substance abuse add to that already bubbling cauldron. Many of the stories I've heard about young adults were heartbreaking. While the drugs I sold were only indicated for adults (18 years old and above), there were always stories shared by the health care professionals I worked with of teens whose brains had been permanently altered by trauma or substance abuse. One of my doctors told me years ago to make sure to keep my boys away from drugs because the chemicals in them can have an adverse effect as they compete with the natural chemicals in their brains. The doctor told me that this can be especially concerning given that young brains are still developing and the "judging and reasoning" part of the brain develops last. This should explain the often-unexplainable behavior our teens sometimes engage in. They simply aren't prepared to make decisions yet and are pre-wired for risky behavior.

Furthermore, most parents are unaware of how our genes interact with our brain's development. We are all impacted by nature **and** nurture as researchers at Harvard University's Center for the Developing Child are rapidly uncovering. "As essential as they are, we aren't born with the skills that enable us to control impulses, make plans, and stay focused. We are born with the potential to develop these capacities - or not - depending on our experiences during infancy, throughout childhood, and into adolescence. Our genes provide the blueprint, but the early environments in which children live leave a lasting signature on those genes. This signature influences how or whether that genetic potential is expressed in the brain circuits that underlie executive function capacities children will rely on throughout their lives[i]."

The term "executive function" refers to the brain's ability to sort and utilize information, tune out things which aren't important, and plan controlled responses to the situations that confront us each day[ii]. Instead of being erratic and impulsive, if our level of executive function is high, we are rational and deliberate in our actions. Executive function is controlled by the prefrontal cortex which covers the frontal lobe of our brains. This area of the cerebrum is the largest part of the human brain and is responsible for thoughts such as reasoning, planning, emotions, problem-solving, and perception. This is where teens are deficient for most of their teenage years, and this is where the infamous prefrontal cortex is housed[iii].

Time Magazine's special issue, *The Science of Childhood*, does a masterful job of explaining what is going on inside the minds of our children during this precarious time of life. Alexandra Sifferlin explains in her article, *Why Teenage Brains Are So Hard to Understand*, "Doctors, parents and teachers have long held preconceived notions about why teenagers act so reckless and emotional, and many of these explanations have turned out to be incorrect. It was once believed that teens were impulsive due to raging hormones and that they were difficult because they hated authority. But advances in brain imaging, which gathered force in the 2000s, told a much more complicated story. It turns out the teenage brain is nowhere near fully baked and that the brain's structure and its effects on development continues into a person's 20s[iv]."

Sifferlin goes on to explain that the actual structure of the teen brain changes, not by getting bigger as it grows, but by strengthening connections between brain regions through the increase of myelin, a fatty substance in the brain which "wraps around" the nerves. "Myelination, the scientific name for this process, strengthens and accelerates the communication between brain regions and underlies a person's basic learning abilities. The myelination process starts from the back of the brain and works its way to the front. That means the prefrontal cortex, the area of the brain involved in decision-making, planning, and self-control, is the last part to mature. It's not that teens don't have frontal- lobe capabilities but rather that their signals are not getting to the back of the brain fast enough to regulate their emotions. It's why risk-taking and impulsive behaviors are more common among teens and young adults."

Do your homework and pick up a copy of this article as well as any others you can find about the teen brain. During this time, even though you may be tired and hormonal yourself, you must be on guard for subtle changes in your child's behavior which are abnormal. Yes, they will be sleepy, irritable, and hard to get along with, but if you sense that something more profound and darker may be attacking them, seek help immediately. Sifferlin brings the issue right to our laps by reminding us of how the brain can malfunction during the teen years. "The teen brain's rapidly growing connections carry some negative side effects. About 70% of mental illnesses, including anxiety, mood and eating disorders, and psychosis, appear in the teen years and early adulthood. The timing makes sense, since the prefrontal cortex and frontal lobes are implicated in the emergence of diseases like depression and schizophrenia. Risks for health issues like addiction are also higher during this time period." In society today, the pressure on teens is greater than ever before. Perfect SAT scores are on the rise, and every kiddo believes that if they aren't Mark Zuckerberg or Kylie Jenner, they are failures - and secretly, many parents believe this as well. Do yourself and your kids a favor, have high expectations but breathe, laugh, and read **Late Bloomers: The Power of Patience in a World Obsessed with Early Achievement** by Rich Karlgaard. No amount of success is worth your child's mental health.

The Teenage Brain, a book by Dr. Frances E. Jensen with Amy Ellis Nutt, also shares intricate insight on your teen and how their brains work. Not only does Dr. Jensen share her first-hand experience with raising two teen boys as a divorced mom, but she also covers our most concerning issues like why our teens sleep so much to tobacco, alcohol, pot, hardcore drugs, and stress. "This book is the classic survival guide to the care and feeding of the teenage brain. Kids brains are her specialty." **The Teenage Brain** taught me how to better handle situations with my boys and enhanced my understanding of why I constantly ask, "What is wrong with them?" One of the reasons I find great value in this book is that it speaks to facts and studies versus parenting "the best way you can." Please pick up a copy; you will not be disappointed.

There are so many reasons why examining the teen brain is crucial for not only menopausal parents, but for all parents in general. It gives us a chance to peek behind the curtain to see a bit of the "why" behind our teens' madness. When your teen can't seem to start a task and stay focused on it to completion, can't ever seem to be on time or keep their room clean, can't seem to self-monitor themselves or regulate their emotions - just know that there is a 13-year-old party going on in their heads. Before you get frustrated and pounce on them, remember that the chaos of teen behavior is somewhat due to underdeveloped executive function. They are driven more by impulsive decision making rather than thoughtful reasoning. Teens need your guidance and support during this period more than ever. They may be less lovable, but the teen years are when they need your love most of all! Somehow my mom broke through the code and managed to help influence the teenagers she worked with years ago and I think it's possible for us moms to do the same. We, the parents, will have to drive this train for our teens until they can take over the wheel. They will ultimately have to learn responsibility and hone the skill sets needed to guide themselves, but we can make a difference in their lives now.

So, what can parents do to help their teens?

1. <u>Keep your teen focused on what they love to do</u>. Keep them busy! My mom put me and my sister in dance at an early age. She allowed us to try several different activities. I was a girl scout, was in 4H, took dance classes, volunteered at church, spoke in the church youth oratorical contest, was in community plays, etc. She kept us extremely busy during our teen years but the one thing that resonated the most with me was dance. I became obsessed with leaps, turns, and execution. The thing I remembered most was how interested mom and dad became in my execution of dance moves. They would watch intently while I practiced and would give me feedback on what I could do better or what was not so great. As I reflect on those days, I felt like they were in it with me. They were invested in my ability to be a great dancer. For hours on end, I would dance, work on leaps, or any area of focus that I needed to execute better. Clearly, I never

had time to get involved in the "risky behavior" that so many young teens got themselves into.

2. <u>Give teens room to get things right</u>. If they have done something wrong and need a consequence, allow room for negotiation. Let them tell you what their punishment should be. Give them a chance to "make it right."

3. <u>Find a trusted mentor for them</u>. Sometimes we are not the best coaches for our kids and are just not equipped with enough information to guide them. Yeah, I know it's hard to read this. Lol! If they are interested in becoming a veterinarian, find a friend who is a veterinarian who can help them navigate that area of interest. Honestly, what can I tell TJ about being a vet? Thank God for my line sister, Dr. LRB. She checks in with TJ once a month to talk to him about veterinarian school, Jr. Vet Camp, his academics, etc. It has been a great experience for him.

4. <u>Seek counseling for your teen</u>. Even the school's guidance counselor is a good place to start. They have great insight into the culture of the school and what kids are dealing with within the walls of your teen's school. Just know that your teen is not the only one that may be having problems, and the school's counselors may have all kinds of ideas as to how to help them.

5. <u>Choose your battles</u>. You have probably heard this many times before, but you need to choose your battles carefully to win the war. One of the psychiatrists I called on long ago as a drug rep told me that the things that are least harmful are okay for teens to explore. Let them dye their hair because hair grows back, let them pierce their ears because the hole will close, let them wear long nails because they can be cut, it's the majors in life that you want to be prepared to fight for.

6. <u>Highlight their accomplishments</u>. Make a big deal of the things they get right! If you want to see more of the positive behaviors they demonstrate, let them know how much of an impact that behavior has made on the whole family. Teens are at a crucial time in their lives when their self-esteem hangs in the balance every waking moment of the day. The more you can validate them, lift them up, and highlight their awesomeness, the more they believe it and live it. Sing their praises to the mountain tops, and you will fill their hearts with confidence!

7. <u>Display their great works</u>. Hang their work or any work of art that reflects who they are. It will show them how proud you are of them and make them feel special.

TJ

LEX

MENOPAUSE VS. PUBERTY

3.

The Balance

September 13, 2012

TJ just walked past me, and the armpit odor nearly knocked me off my chair! I said, "TiJuan, go wash under your arms!"

He said, "It's okay, Mom, that's my intimidation factor for football practice tonight. It's okay, really!" ...WTH?!!!

October 3, 2014

After a thorough discussion with my eight-year-old son regarding hygiene, "I will wash you from head to toe myself if you don't get this thing right 'cuz I can't take your smelly butt not one minute longer!"

Later that day after said eight-year-old took a shower, "Mom,

I'm done bathing, and I did a great job! I even washed between my toes this time!"

I'm not sure how I'm surviving this.

~~~

Many moms have the benefit of working from home or not working traditional "office" jobs. Some moms even have time to get to the gym every day. For one whole year, I was a "stay-at-home" mom and loved every minute of it. I would do it again in a heartbeat. I loved the freedom of being accessible to my kids physically and emotionally on a more consistent basis. Life had an ease to it, and I enjoyed the fact that I had the internal and external calmness and freedom that I found difficult to experience when I was employed. Every part of my being was available to my boys, and it was not forced. If I'm honest, that was the first time as a mom that I had ever felt such freedom before. That was the point in my life when I could take a deep breath and have the balance I longed for. When I was working full time, I made balance work by force. "Unemployed balance" was like being released from captivity.

I wish I could say I'd planned this awesome vacation from life but, unfortunately, it came as the result of being laid off from my pharmaceutical sales position after 20+ years of employment. Here's the funny thing - this employer provided employees with the time and opportunity to interview for other positions within the company. I went on the interviews but was interviewing for pomp and circumstance. Secretly, I was hoping and praying that I wouldn't find another position. I loved the flexibility of not working. I loved the freedom of working out and not having to squeeze it into another part of my day or rushing right out of the gym after I finished. I also enjoyed volunteering at my boys' school and being home to greet them when they arrived each day after school. Who wouldn't?

During the time that I should have been looking for a new position, my manager could not understand my lack of motivation to move through the interview process more quickly. He would say, "You're the only one that doesn't have a sense of urgency around this. Why is that?" I can't remember how I responded, but I refused to be rushed and I think it drove the entire management team crazy. They had deadlines to meet to fill open positions for displaced employees, and I was dreaming of a stress-free life designed for me by me. All I knew was that I didn't want to make a hasty decision. I tried to be happy and excited about yet another "sales rep role" (sigh). Having been put in this situation by unemployment, I now had the luxury of paving a new path and the freedom to do so. Many seemed worried that I wasn't worried enough, and I found that amusing. My truth? I loved being a "stay-at-home-mom" because that's the only time I truly felt I had total balance in my life.

I've been a single parent and I'm currently a married mom with two boys. In both experiences, I've worked a full-time job most of the time. "Balance" or as I call it "suffering in silence" is relative. I imagine that many moms "*SIS.*" It's that unspoken, limitless dedication of stretching ourselves thin to take care of our family, church, friends, and social obligations. So, we push through nausea to make sure our kid makes it to the store to pick up supplies for that school project that they told us about the night before. We rush out to the grocery store to grab food for the field trip the next day because we didn't realize that they'd eaten the supply of snacks we had available in the pantry several days prior. For most of us moms, when you factor in homework, extra-curricular activities like football and basketball, piano and voice lessons, auditions, doctor, dentist and orthodontist appointments, and haircuts our time is spent twice! As a full-time employee and mom, when do you fit in working out, cleaning your home, and grocery shopping?

We warrior parents often laugh at the term "balance" - especially those of us who are (or have been) single parents. For ten years, I struggled to find that "balance" as a single mom. I had heard many high-level female executives speak of how they achieved "balance" at corporate forums at work. They talked about how doable it was and they'd tell us how they achieved it. I'd leave the Q&A session thinking "sure it's doable when you can afford the tandem nanny, house cleaning crew, and student Uber driver to ensure that your kids get to appointments after school. The prospect of THAT "life of balance" was a pipe dream and was not realistic for us common folk. Still, I had false hope. Friends and coworkers often ask me, "How do you balance it all?" My answer is, "I fake it until I make it." I get asked that question a lot and I remember back when I was a single parent it seemed like a regular curiosity for many. I've never really stopped to put words around it, but I think I've always just done what was required with no excuses to get things done. I've always felt the pressure of that old adage "If I don't do it, it won't get done." So, I press forward with a "don't stop, can't stop" mindset and the work, chores, etc. miraculously get done…. or not. Imagine that? For me, I achieve balance when I feel the least pressure about all the things I must accomplish in one day and find time to nurture, validate, and love my kids, and get spillover work done in the evenings.

Forcing balance is certainly not the best approach to getting things accomplished. I often do so at the expense of my mental and physical wellbeing. I'm an overachiever, and I like to see the immediate results of my labor. I think this mindset can sabotage my best efforts. My typical approach is to put my head down and plow through the tasks to make sure they all get done. Do I often feel guilt and frustration when I can't get it all done? Yes. Do I ever say "F— it, I'm tired - this just might not get done?" Yep! Sometimes I will even push past coherency to see the task through to the end no matter what it takes, and then the worst happens - I drop the ball. Just recently TJ and Lex had an orthodontist appointment at 4:30. I hadn't realized that it was 5:00 pm until the doctor's office called to see why we were not there. Now you must understand, these are coveted appointments. They are typically booked out for three to four months. You can't just miss a brace adjustment and expect to get right back on their calendar within the next week. Not to mention that a contortionist act is required on my part to get two appointments for the boys rescheduled around travel schedules, work, other doctor appointments, and practices with minimal disruption to their classes and my job. The older I get, the harder it is to maintain my ability to juggle it all. When you combine the occasional menopausal rages, hot flashes, and headaches, you've got the perfect launching pad for a missile. It's not like me to lose control of my calendar or schedule, and I thrive on the idea that I could be Superwoman, but in truth, I often feel more overwhelmed than balanced and then I punish myself mentally for letting the people I love down.

The truth will set you free - balance for a busy mom is difficult to achieve. I have had to make many temporary sacrifices to make small advances forward. For anyone hoping to find it, I would say that balance is relative to your unique situation and what you and your family have deemed the most essential goals to accomplish. *I believe I find balance by choosing what's most important at the time and focusing my best efforts there.* To be clear, I will not allow the lack of balance to get in the way of my family's progress. For example, currently, the boys are preparing for their annual Christmas piano concert. It is in three weeks and they haven't been practicing as much as they should due to loads of homework, basketball practice, basketball games, agility training, and auditions. Did I mention that neither of them has had a haircut in over four weeks? Please make a note here, that I absolutely live for "hair cut day." I will even post the occasional pic to celebrate the "fresh cut" moment. It's somewhat silly, but I'm absolutely okay with it. "Hair cut day" is one of the small things in my life that gives me the greatest joy. It makes them look like I care about their appearance and hygiene even when they don't. So, to strike a balance between their busy schedules and getting practice in on the piano, I insist that they squeeze piano practice in twice a day for the next two weeks before their performance. This means that even if we get home at 11:00 pm, they will squeeze in a non-negotiable 15-minute practice on the piano before they go to bed. It is imperative that they get on that stage on "Concert Day" and execute a flawless performance even if it kills us all! So yeah, I call squeezing every bit of what you can in, when you can, without missing deadlines for the good of greatness "balance."

Tips on creating balance:

1. What are your goals and priorities as a family? Call a family meeting and decide what each member wants to accomplish and how. For kids, it's important to know what they must sacrifice (or what the family must sacrifice) to get it done.

2. Take a deep breath because some things will fall through the cracks and not get done despite your best efforts. Choose your poison. If clean laundry must sit for a week to get the cleaning done in the bathroom, I'll choose the clean toilet over putting clothes away every time hands down.

3. Get your kids to own some of the responsibility. I've had to work really hard at not being "the hand that everyone fans with."

I recently realized that I've become an enabler in my efforts to be a "good" mom. I'm learning to get out of their way and let them figure it out. Make a list of what you want and need them to help you with and have them check items off as they complete the tasks.

4. If there are one or two things that would make your heart happy when you walk in the door from work, teach your kids to do it early in life!" I love it when my kids get right to their homework when they get home from school/practice. I don't have to ask them to do it and they don't argue about not wanting to do it. They were taught this at an early age and it has become a habit.

5. Know what's most important for your kids to accomplish and only spend time on those things. (With certain extracurriculars there will always be non-negotiables i.e. for me - playing the piano.)

6. Don't be afraid to ask for help.

MENOPAUSE VS. PUBERTY

4.

The Truth

1985

Kelsie's response to getting into trouble for doing something she wasn't supposed to when she was four: "Mommy, don't say "bad Kelsie" say "bad hand."

Me: "Whose hand is it, Booba?"

October 11, 2014

We were set up and ambushed! We were all riding along in the car tonight and TJ says, "I know that you and mom are the tooth fairy....my tooth has been under my pillow for the last two days and nothing happened."

A few days later, TJ came downstairs and said to me, "Mom, I got $2 from the Daddy Tooth Fairy. (I'm tired of TiJuan M. Lumpkin, Sr. getting credit for my work, but I can't divulge *our secret dealings with the tooth fairy, so I say nothing and continue to listen.) Y'all aren't fooling me! In fact, I've been doing some research, and I know who's moving the elf on the shelf, too!"*

I, thinking quickly...'cuz I'm stealthy like that, proceed to divert him from further convincing himself of mine and T's sneaky dealings by doing the only thing I know how to do...redirect and divert!!! So, I say, "Boy, is that a booger stuck to your face? How many times have I told you to wash your face when you wake up in the morning? Go clean yourself up!" So, I kiss him on the booger-less side of his face and send him back upstairs to wash up!

Yep, safe to say I got this parenting thing down!!!! Anyone need advice?

~ ~ ~

The truth is like water trapped in the crevice of a rock. It will always find its way out.

-T-Lisa-ism

Being honest with my kids has sometimes been a challenge. We lied like most parents about the tooth fairy, Santa, Elf on the Shelf, and the Easter Bunny. Admittedly, I've also stretched other truths to persuade my kids to do the right thing. For example, there was the time when we realized that allowing the boys to play video games may not have been the best decision, so to limit them, I lied. I told them that it was a proven fact that evolution would cause their thumbs to adapt to their video-playing habit and that by the time they became adults their thumbs would be longer than their other fingers. Then there was the time that I convinced them that I had eyes in the back of my head. The truth is, I got lucky because I could see their reflection in a well-placed glass vase at the time. I'm also not ashamed of the time I told my son that kissing girls would make his lips swell. He looked at me as if to say, "No way...but...could that *really* happen?" That's when I said "You can't go kissing just any old random girl. Do you remember the princess and the frog story? Well, do you want to be a frog?" My all-time favorite was the time I told the boys that the best place to find a wife was in a nursing home in their twilight years of life. "That's where I would start," I said.

Needless to say, these lies were entertaining for me but not so much for the boys. I've used these lies to teach them two things - that they can't believe everything people tell them and that people can see through their lies. I also want them to know that you should never take yourself so seriously that you miss out on the best moments in life. Most of all, I love their laughter. Their initial facial expressions upon hearing my outlandish responses are everything. We laugh a lot in our family.

Having parenting experience with three teenagers doesn't make me an expert; it just means I've had three practice runs at getting this parenting thing right. Between the boys constantly getting caught being 13 and 14 and my low level of tolerance and patience, let's just say they don't usually want to hear the truth from me. However, there are far too many negative consequences if we aren't brutally honest with our kids. They will search for the real answers out there in the world, and I'm not willing to gamble on who they will get their answers from and how those responses will impact their lives. I fear that they could find the wrong answers in all the wrong places. Having the courage to tell them things they might not want to hear and dealing with the complaints that you are being mean can be difficult, **but it is imperative that you tell them the truth anyway**. This becomes even harder when they become young adults. It is then that they start thinking they know more than you and start listening to their friends. This thought process breeds peer pressure and experimentation. You cannot prevent outside influences from creeping into their lives. For this reason, teaching them at an early age to tell the truth, find their own answers, and to be honest, is important.

My mom and dad had a powerful "truth serum" - WORK! They kept us so busy in activities and physical movement that we never had idol time for mischief which in turn gave us fewer opportunities to do things that we might have to lie about. My mom also believed strongly in the philosophy, "don't ever put your kids in a position to lie to you." She'd tell me, "Don't ask if Kelsie's done the thing in question. If you know she did it, move right to the conversation of how she is going to make the thing right." An example that I remember was when Kelsie was about five. She wrote on my mom's bedspread. It was obvious to us all that she had done it. It was her "little person handwriting" and she was the only child in the house. I called her into mom's room to show her. When I ask her if she'd written on Grammy's bed, of course, she said no. Mom was present so when Kelsie left the room, she asked me, "Do you see how that's a no-way-out situation? You are frustrated, you are no closer to the truth of what happened, and Kelsie has no consequence and thinks she has gotten away with it." Mom was right, and I felt all those feelings. She then said to me, "In the future say to Kel, "I know you wrote on mom's bed. This is not okay. You will apologize to Grammie and Granddaddy and next time you will ask for paper to write on instead." I had so much to learn.

Most of what I've read about raising honest kids says that "all kids lie." They are no different from adults in that they don't want to hurt anyone's feelings, they don't want to get into trouble, and they want to puff themselves up in front of their friends. What I've learned in my research is that **parents must first model telling the truth and never set their kids up to manufacture a lie**. Also, parents should speak positively about their kids and make a big deal of it when they tell the truth. My parents were pros at this.

Everything I learned at a young age, about telling the truth is centered around my parents' strict rules. There were harsh penalties for lying and we learned to just not do it. I try to be honest with everyone - young or old - even today and even when it's hard. Being honest with my kids can be painful at times. I can see the hurt in their eyes when I tell them something they don't want to hear. I don't advocate being mean for no reason, but I believe in tough love. It's important for my boys to have an accurate assessment of themselves. I try to teach them to do the right thing and to be honest at all costs. Kids learn by example, so we as parents must be their template. We must be honest even when it hurts and even when we're embarrassed. I live by one of William Shakespeare's most famous lines from Hamlet, "This above all, to thine own self be true, and it must follow as the night the day, thou canst not be false to anyone."

At some point in life the light bulb comes on, and you realize that being honest and straightforward is the best thing you can do for yourself, your family, your friends, and acquaintances. I will admit it's not always easy, but it certainly does weed out a lot of BS from your life. I can't tell you the number of times I've told people right up front "absolutely not" or "listen, don't send me the video or any information on that product because I'm not interested." It's not mean, it's just setting your boundaries while being very transparent and honest. It also cuts down the constant text messages and inbox questions like, "Have you read it yet, did you like it, or will you use it?"

Growing up, I watched my parents sacrifice so much for my sister and me. I'd also been exposed to peers whose parents weren't so invested in their kids' lives and had seen firsthand the damage lying could do to young minds. At first, I wasn't sure what I wanted to invest in my kids but when I became a parent for the first time, I understood why my parents made such sacrifices for my sister and me. Just think - parents are given one of the most crucial responsibilities of raising, influencing, and shaping young minds with little to no experience, coupled with the freedom to lie to their kids at will about any and everything. Parents are given full control with no prior preparation, little accountability, minimal positive examples, and no training. This can, in some instances, be a recipe for disaster.

For example, I often think of the day my mom told my sister, then 2, and me, 7, about her friend, Ms. Judy. Ms. Judy's grandfather raised her to believe that all black people had tails. Mom had tears in her eyes as she told us the story and warned us that it is never good to lie because it can sometimes be fatal. We knew and loved Ms. Judy as she and mom were the closest of friends, and I remember laughing at how silly Ms. Judy was and wondered if her Granddaddy had ever gone to school. Surely, he would not have thought such a silly thing if he had been an educated man. That story stayed with me as it was not only inconceivable, it was hurtful, and I, at a young age, learned the importance of always telling the truth. Honesty and truth helped me to fight through insecurities and to stand boldly and assertively in the face of lies. How could anyone tell or believe such an ugly lie?

Lying parents create and nurture a vicious cycle of pain and insecurity within their children. We currently live in a society that seems to embrace lies and twisted truths and hurt people hurt people. The constant physical and emotional abuse of children is not only cruel and negligent, but it is also unthinkable and unforgivable as it impacts all of mankind.

Children manifest emotional abuse and distrust of adults in many ways. Does your kiddo lie or speak disrespectfully to adults? Are they moody or generally hard to get along with? Is there a medical or psychological reason for what your child is doing? I don't offer this advice lightly or callously, but don't be afraid to ask your pediatrician if your child does things that disturb you and you don't know why. The truth is, you must be honest with yourself about your child's disposition. We've seen firsthand the devastation of the school shootings, suicides, and depression that plague young people today because someone failed to notice that things weren't right.

Mental, behavioral, and developmental disorders begin in early childhood - sometimes even as young as three. One in six U.S. children between the ages of two and eight years old (17.4%) had a diagnosed mental, behavioral, or developmental disorder. It's important to note that with each new birthday, new problems could pop up that you hadn't noticed or dealt with before. For example, behavior problems are more common in children between the ages of 6 and 11, and depression and anxiety become more common with age. There are certain problems your child may grow out of, or into right under your watchful eye, so don't be afraid to seek help and do your research to understand exactly what is going on! If talking to your pediatrician isn't helpful, there is a wealth of information out there and people dedicated to helping families. The National Institute for Mental Health provides information on children and mental health including how to identify it, where to seek help, treatment options, and more[v].

Honesty starts with you. It's sometimes challenging for parents to face the truth of what's really going on with their children. It can feel lonely and dredge up major insecurities. When kids are struggling with something that's noticeable to others, snide remarks and judgmental comments may also make it difficult to seek help. While it may be uncomfortable to realize that your child is struggling with something hard - hiding your head in the sand or just defending your child won't help. If you aren't honest, they won't be either. You must face the truth and help them face the truth so that you will raise a child who is honest and whole. And - believe it or not - you will feel so much better when you realize that there is help available and that others are going through what you're going through. It can so often seem like everyone in the world is perfect except for you, but the truth is there are no perfect parents or perfect children.

These "truths" will bless you:

1. Thomas Carlyle once said, "Make thyself a better person and, by that, you can be sure that there is one less rascal in the world." I believe the same is true for parenting, "Make thyself an honest parent and, by that, you can be sure to raise one less rascal in the world." Lol!

2. Watch and learn from your kids - you are responsible for cultivating their superpowers!

3. Encourage them to be "GREAT," not just good or not just "their personal best!" Trust me. They are far greater than they know or believe they are!

4. Stop telling them and show them! (Oh my God, this is the toughest one for me because I love to cuss - it seems to put the right emphasis on what I'm trying to convey. It sprinkles a

little seasoning on my words, but I'm trying not to raise kids who cuss, so I have to watch it!)

5. Beat them unmercifully in competition (in any game or foot race). They need a measure to strive for and a will to achieve it!

6. Become who you want your kids to be! When we become adults, we suck at a lot of things, carry around our insecurities from childhood, and tend to be stubborn and set in our ways! FIX IT!

7. APOLOGIZE to them when you have made a mistake or misjudged their actions. You are not superhuman, and they need to know it! This is one of the best ways to model how to tell the truth.

8. Stand up for them with a mighty force when they are right and bring the wrath down on them when they are wrong! They will deal with a consequence either way and learn that every action has a consequence.

9. Do not let them disrespect others to promote their own agenda as you will indeed be cultivating an ass! (Psst....you are not hiding anything when you do this. People say nothing, but they see through you and will surely disconnect from the donkey you have raised.)

10. I have said this one before and will continue to shout it from the rooftops. Hell, I could write a whole book on this one alone! (This is #17 of the 50-year-old learnings I posted when I turned 50.) We ALL think our children are GREAT...and THEY ALL ARE! Not just

yours, damn it!!! (See how that curse word added a little spice to my point?)

I'll stop here, but I'm far from done! Lol!

Speak the truth even if your voice shakes, even if it's hard, even if you need help to tell the truth. Recognizing the pitfalls and continuous parent traps of saying "no" but still giving in, or seeing a potential problem brewing but turning the blind eye because you want peace, or you are just not up for the "fight," are not viable options. The next step is working towards solutions to make yourself an honest parent. It's okay not to want to have the talks, fight the battles, and admit medical flaws, but you must come back around at some point and face them head on - the consequences of not addressing the issues are too costly.

5.

The Job

January 7, 2018

Me: Fussing at this point because I had had enough! "Lex, didn't I ask you to practice the piano? Why am I still not hearing any music? Ms. Martha will be here in a few days. How is it gonna' look if you don't have your notes together?" I waited because there was no music coming from the piano room.

Lex: "You have reached the voicemail of Lex Lumpkin. I'm sorry I can't take your call right now. Please leave a message after the beep and I will call you back as soon as possible. Beeeep!"

After a moment of total silence he began to play…'cuz yeah, I was on my way to the voice recorder….no words were needed at this point.

I think he got this from his Dad. I had way too much work to do to keep fooling around with him.

~~~

"Sorry for the mean, awful, accurate things I said."
-ENTJ Humor

Many moms are working at least two full-time jobs every day. The one they get a paycheck for and the one they don't. Wives and mothers are rewarded by the sheer joy and life fulfillment that comes from their children, spouses, and homes. There is nothing like seeing your little ones jumping for joy the minute you walk into the daycare at the end of a workday to take them home. These are the moments we live for and which somehow make the chaos of juggling both positions worthwhile. To be successful at both, however, you must learn how to overcome chaos and commit to "getting it done" in the eye of the storm. This requires resilience, intestinal fortitude, and an ability to push past any roadblock that gets in your way no matter how impenetrable it may seem. Getting to the gym and fitting in your workout at 11:00 PM after you've completed spreadsheets for work and put the kids to bed is a great example. Another is staying up till 3:00 AM making pirate sails, sashes, and banners in an effort to try to "Disney-up" your kid's birthday party. You get the impossible done because mountains are movable right? I call it "digging deep!" Deep into that realm of "I can push myself further" and the "no matter what, I'll get it done." We will touch on this more later in the book.

As a note of caution to MVP readers, I am driven. You may have noticed that from my aforementioned thoughts on parenting. I have a need to succeed. Armed with a BS from Tuskegee University and an MBA from the University of Tennessee, I hit the ground running in my career. In my 23 years of sales experience, I have reached both exemplary rating status and a #1 sales rank. I was extremely fortunate to have had the opportunity to work for some of the best and most well-known organizations throughout my career including Revlon, the NFL, and Eli Lilly. I worked for a Fortune 500 Company for over 20 years. Five of those years I worked in HR representing the sales and marketing teams, and the other 15-18 years in Field Sales. I have been named District MVP more than once. One thing I learned quickly from these years of experience is that no matter the culture, no matter how difficult to navigate within, you must control your narrative. Don't look to someone else to tell your story.

During my HR days, I'd coach reps to control their days with their managers during field ride-alongs. A "ride-along" in sales is when a Pharma sales manager spends two days out in the field with each representative. These could be days from the very pit of hell or absolutely awesome days, but it totally depended on the rep. These moments are crucial when you are trying to get promoted. I'd often coach reps not to wait for their managers to ask them all the questions on field ride-along days, but rather to be ready to tell their managers what they could expect to see throughout the day, how they've improved upon an area of development, and what their expectations are of their managers. I'd tell them to remind their managers at the beginning of the day what their deliverables were from the last visit and show them how you've improved on those deliverables. If you want my advice, *be a constant contributor.* Think of ways to level up your contributions and bend them to your will.

I try to step back, evaluate everything, and assess the best approach given the time I have available and how I want the final presentation to look. I often spend way too much time thinking about the different ways to get a task done. For me, it's never a win/lose. I don't view things that way. It can *always* be a win, it just depends on the value you put on the solution. It's like putting a giant puzzle together with several tiny pieces. You know that it might take hours to locate the exact puzzle piece that fits in a certain section of your puzzle, but you also know that every piece will eventually fit if you just stay with it. The outcome, a clear picture for you to enjoy and relish, makes the pain of putting it together worth it. The rush I get from the completion of a difficult project, or from figuring out how to get a skeptical provider to prescribe my product is indescribable. My greatest motivator is when I've been told, "It can't be done," "We've never done it that way before," or "Why waste your time there?"

Although I was successful at what I did, during those years I wanted desperately to be in sales training. No matter who I networked with, despite countless special projects, and no matter how many hoops I jumped through, I couldn't quite get the supporters. I've had two roles within the same company where I performed so well that I was held back from promotions. I found this puzzling but true fact out later when management changed, and new managers were hired. That was a hard lesson - others were telling my story and misrepresenting me. It's unfortunate, but it happens. *All working mothers need to control their own narratives.*

This was a major learning opportunity for me. There were several times in my career that being a mom took precedence over any decision I made about my "work life" and many times when my "home life" suffered also. I remember once during an early morning jog before work, I cried the whole six-mile distance. I cried because I felt used at work and not valued, and I cried because I'd made sacrifices in my personal life that were unfair to my family. I was frustrated because I knew that despite my hard work and long hours at the office, I might not get the result or promotion I wanted. This happens to many moms. Employers "write us off" because we aren't perceived as capable of making it to the next level. In the minds of many, we working moms are still considered a "risky hire" so we must learn to work hard and prove our worth without sacrificing our families. *Pursuing my dreams at the expense of my children was not an option for me.* This was a difficult pill to swallow because I am accustomed to winning it all and having it all.

I have an extreme passion for my goals and want to be very successful when I know I am dealing with a difficult product. I love to hear people say, "Wow!" That passion for reaching goals that are perceived to be unreachable is what drives me. I like to achieve what people say I can't. It was the same thing with my body. People told me I would never lose the baby weight - but I did! People told me I would never run a marathon - but I did! My dad instilled this in me. He always challenged us. He would say, "Lisa, I bet you can't beat me running to that tree!" I would think, "I'll show him!" A lot of people are comfortable setting the goal, but don't consider what it will take to achieve it. Winning takes sacrifice and commitment. To reach your goals, you must be ready for a new level of mental strength. Sacrifice is tough. It requires the bending of your will.

Then there are those days that just don't cooperate with me. One morning I got up early for work to get a workout in. After 45 minutes on the elliptical, I headed for the shower. While in the shower, every smoke detector in our home went off at the same time! I started running around the house grabbing my ears because the noise was sooo loud. I called 911 and they told me to get out of the house and stay there until the fire department came. All these thoughts ran through my mind:

"I can't get out of the house! I'm not "fire-department-ready!""

"I wonder if I can clean up the kitchen before they get here?"

"Is that jelly on the counter? Damn it, why didn't the boys clean up after breakfast?"

"The kitchen is a mess...maybe they won't notice!"

"I hate my kids!"

"Oh sh*t, am I gonna' die by fire today, Jesus?"

"Where is my hat? My head is a mess!"

"Why the hell does this always happen to me?"

"I hate T (hubby), too!"

Here I am trying to grab and hide my titties, mad cause my house is a mess, not sure if it was gonna' explode, and torn between getting out of the house half-dressed or taking time to clean the kitchen. There were just too many other decisions to make! Needless to say, there was no smoke or fire. The firemen said that some wires could have shorted out and they should be replaced. Thank God! I swore it was my husband's fault! My "near-death" experience was of no consequence to him, because when I called him to tell him what happened, I got the standard "I'm in a meeting" text! Sigh. Yeah, I made this about T. No one was hurt during this fiasco, thank God, and I remember debating purchasing a tiny house just for me. By the time I headed out the door for work, I could have sworn that life was out to get me. Do you ever have those days where you just want to go back home and start the day over again? Too bad we can't "reboot" life.

Both of my jobs collide and co-mix constantly. When you add in my Myers Briggs Personality Type, watch out! I've taken this test at least five times throughout my career in Pharma Sales and across three different companies and my results have always been ENTJ - The Commander.

"ENTJs are natural-born leaders. People with this personality type embody the gifts of charisma and confidence, and project authority in a way that draws crowds together behind a common goal. But unlike their Feeling (F) counterpart, ENTJs are characterized by an often ruthless level of rationality, using their drive, determination, and sharp minds to achieve whatever end they've set for themselves. Perhaps it is best that they make up only three percent of the population, lest they overwhelm the more timid and sensitive personality types that make up much of the rest of the world – but we have ENTJs to thank for many of the businesses and institutions we take for granted every day.

"If there's anything ENTJs love, it's a good challenge, big or small, and they firmly believe that given enough time and resources, they can achieve any goal. This quality makes people with the ENTJ personality type brilliant entrepreneurs, and their ability to think strategically and hold a long-term focus while executing each step of their plans with determination and precision makes them powerful business leaders. This determination is often a self-fulfilling prophecy, as ENTJs push their goals through with sheer willpower where others might give up and move on, and their extraverted (E) nature means they are likely to push everyone else right along with them, achieving spectacular results in the process. At the negotiating table, be it in a corporate environment or buying a car, ENTJs are dominant, relentless, and unforgiving. This isn't because they are cold-hearted or vicious per se – it's more that ENTJ personalities genuinely enjoy the challenge, the battle of wits, the repartee that comes from this environment, and if the other side can't keep up, that's no reason for ENTJs to fold on their own core tenet of ultimate victory."

My happiness, as I mentioned, lies totally in the joy of achievement. I take this attitude with me into every area of my life from work, to parenting, to marriage. *The problem is that victory is not always possible in every area at the same time without the relentless pursuit of excellence and driving yourself to live at the highest level at all times.* We're human! We make mistakes, we run out of gas, we forget things, we MUST rest. Life is hard sometimes, and we will all find that we can't keep all the balls in the air at the same time.

For a working mother, there will never be complete balance, but you can learn to perform at such a high level at work that your presence is invaluable. In doing so, you will earn the grace you need when your family needs you. Do everything you can to be memorable and irreplaceable at work, and you will excel. Be excellent in all that you do but don't be surprised if your boss wants to keep you instead of letting you spread your wings and fly. When you find your norm amid the chaos, you can excel. Work will always be there, it will always be hectic, and you can always be replaced. There is peace within the eye of the storm. Find that intense part and learn to live in it.

T'Lisa's Tips for Being a Great Employee

1. Build relationships. Do you really know your customers as individuals? Do you care? Why is it important to know what they like and dislike, how they think, what they think about you, and how you spend their time when you have it? If you aren't in sales, ask yourself the same question about your boss or immediate supervisor.

2. Expect to win!. When you walk like a winner and look like a winner, people believe that you are a winner. When you have a positive attitude and confidence about winning, you shape people's perceptions of you. Your actions and contributions speak volumes.

3. Know thy self. What is your level of ability? Do you have what it takes to be a water walker? What are you willing to give or give up? How are you viewed by your peers? Be honest with yourself and ask these questions – who am I? Do I have integrity? Do I know how to admit when I mess up? In my profession, if you aren't self-aware and honest with self, you won't do well. I worked in HR and had conversations with people where they couldn't get past their own misguided perceptions of themselves. One person will fill a cup with different sized rocks and balls and some people don't leave room for the sand.

4. Control your narrative. Don't leave your story to someone else to tell for you. Decide what you want

people to know about you and shape their perception of you. Discover how you will make it happen and what tools you'll need to implement your plan and deliver it! Make sure that you deserve your status. When your peers believe in you, trust you and see you as a leader that is one of the most rewarding accomplishment you can achieve at work. This, in my opinion, is the highest marker of success because your peers are the toughest on you. They expect you to bring your "A-game" to work every day for the betterment of the team, and they should! There is no "I" in TEAM. Top performers have figured out that it takes a "when I win, we all win" mentality to be successful. And besides, who wants to work with the doorknob teammate that you have to drag around on your back to get the job done every day? No one!!!!

5. Know your stuff! Be extremely knowledgeable of the material you are expected to deliver. Do your research and understand your customers and competitors. Make sure you know what you need to know and constantly challenge yourself on what you don't know. Be honest when you don't have all the answers but make sure you know the answer on that next visit.

6.

The Divorce

November 3, 2011

Moment of clarity – "I have two baby's daddies!!!!" TJ decided to ask me if Daddy was Kelsie's dad. I said no, that she had a different dad. Well, he proceeds to think through this awkward situation and I just got more uncomfortable as the moments passed. He wanted to know how this all happened and aren't you supposed to only marry one person, when did you and daddy get married, and where is Kelsie's daddy now, etc........ Lesson learned: ONLY GET MARRIED ONE TIME!!!!!!

~~~

Divorce is hardest on the children. There are an enormous amount of studies and articles out there that outline the pitfalls of divorce and what happens to kids when they fall victim to broken marriages. Before you slam down this book and call me judgmental, please know that I'm not berating parents with this tidbit of information - I've been married twice myself. I'm just sharing my experience and honest thoughts in the hope that others may benefit from my mistakes.

If you can stay together, *by all means, do*! Prayer changes things and people. With that being said, if you find yourself already divorced, I offer you the advice I recently gave to a friend - no matter what, DO NOT ALLOW GUILT to creep into your heart. I felt guilty for years about raising my now 29-year-old daughter as a child of divorce, but the truth is, I made the best decision I could at the time. By taking her out of a toxic environment I intended to teach her, by example, that life could be happy, that people should not be arguing and fighting constantly, and that a relationship between two people in love is worth having and working for. Leave all the old baggage at the old location, Sis. When you move forward, do so with a positive mindset. I drug my baggage around with me for ten years, and it was demeaning and exhausting. I did not have the tools to help my daughter or to get through one of the most turbulent times of our lives back then, but I'm here to tell you that *you will survive this,* and your life can be beautiful after a divorce.

My parents got married on April 21, 1963, and have been married for 57 years and counting. My sister and I are so proud of their commitment and dedication to their union. I've always had an awesome relationship with them and consider myself one of the fortunate ones to have had a great childhood full of love and healthy nurturing. While no marriage is perfect, my parents were an exceptional example for me. I entered my marriage armed and ready for success - or so I thought.

I got married at a very young age, in my opinion, and for the wrong reasons, but the birth of my daughter Kelsie was by far the best thing to happen during our eight years of marriage. I was 25 years old when I had her, and she was absolutely beautiful. Kel not only stole my heart but also my mom, dad, and sister's. I'll never forget the first time Kelsie and I traveled to Florida to spend time with my parents. They met us at the gate. I walked down the terminal holding my beautiful baby. As we entered the airport entrance, my Mom swooped out of nowhere, whisked the baby right out of my arms, and she and Dad started walking ahead of me in the direction of baggage claim cooing and ogling at baby Kelsie. This was their very first grandbaby and they were the perfect grandparents. Both belted a quick, "Hey, Lisa!" my way and kept walking ahead with my baby. Like many new mothers, I felt like a host or a carrier who could totally disappear and no one would notice. Finally, I yelled ahead, "Can a sista' get a hug? Something? I did all the work you know! It was only 26 hours of labor!"

Despite the joy surrounding Kelsie's birth, dark days lie ahead. Her father and I would divorce just a few years after this joyful moment leaving Kelsie to become another statistic of divorce. Although we were still in her life, the pain of living between two worlds left a startling effect on her. No one tells you while you are going through it, but divorce changes children forever. No matter how hard we parents try, children are left with scars that will never heal. My only goal at the onset of the breakup of my marriage was to bring some peace to my daughter's life as quickly as possible. Here is where the guilt began. I wanted the life for Kelsie that I'd had growing up. I did not want her to be a statistic of divorce. Kelsie was three years old at the time her father and I separated, and it seemed like we had spent most of her waking moments arguing in front of her. I couldn't remember seeing my parents argue a lot growing up. In fact, most of my memories as a kid through high school are filled with happy times and loads of laughter. I kept thinking to myself, "this is not the life my daughter deserves."

Reflecting on my life back then, I think we just had different goals. We got married too young and too soon. I married the first person I had sex with out of guilt because I was raised to believe that you don't have sex until after you're married. I guess my young adult ideals often conflicted with how I was raised - not in a rebellious way but more in an inquisitive one. "Would God really judge me if I didn't go to church every Sunday or every Bible study on Wednesday night?" These were just a few questions whirling around in my thoughts. When the realization that I married because I was looking for a way to be free from my guilt coupled with hearing that "college" is where you meet your husband, I agreed to marry my first husband rather hastily and under misguided assumptions.

Our worlds and perspective on life would prove to be drastically different. I wanted to pursue my master's degree, move from a two-bedroom co-op to a home and relocate to an area of the country that was not as fast-paced as New York City, and he didn't. Don't get me wrong. I had a lot of fun times living there. Taking classes at the Alvin Ailey School of Dance and the

Broadway Dance Center, working at Revlon and the NFL, runway modeling, and dancing in music videos were some of the many highlights of living in New York, but once my daughter was born I did not want to raise her in such a crazy environment. Having lived in Florida all my life, NYC was a beast to navigate for me day-to-day with a young baby.

The strain of an irreconcilable marriage coupled with daily life in "The Big Apple" eventually got the best of me. Two events (among many others) nudged me to pack up and throw in the towel. One morning I had to get my then newborn, Kelsie, to the pediatrician. Because of the parking rules, you had to park on a designated side of the street on alternating days. So, imagine pushing the baby stroller two or three blocks in the dead of winter only to get to your car and find that someone has double-parked next to you blocking you in. Since the passenger side of my car was damaged from having been hit while parked on a prior day, I had to wedge myself between my car and the double-parked car to try to open the door behind the driver's seat to open the window just enough to slide my baby into the car to get her out of the elements. Once I got the stroller in the trunk of the car, I then had to do the very same maneuver to get to the driver's side of the car and then climb through the window to start the car to try to get it warm inside. Then I had to wait after blowing the horn forever for the person who had double-parked and blocked me in to come out to move his car. To top it all off, he was angry with me for blowing my horn so ferociously. By now I'm incensed and indignant! Needless to say, I was extremely late to the pediatrician's office. Much of life there for me with a baby was tough. Dragging strollers on buses and trains to get from one destination to the other was not the life for me.

The second event was the time I was home during maternity leave right before Kelsie was born. There was the constant sound of someone beating and dragging a body in the apartment above ours every day. With wood flooring, it was impossible to escape the screaming and loud rumbling noises over my head. It got so bad one day that I snapped. I was home on maternity leave. It was just a few days before Kelsie was born. I was startled out of sleep by one of the worst fights I'd heard between the two people above us. It was very disturbing for me, and I remember feeling several emotions rush by me. I was afraid for the woman who seemed to be a constant victim of abuse, and I was angry because she wouldn't stop him from attacking her (I realize now that many women are too afraid to fight back in the face of their abusers). I was also angry that this experience was now a part of my life. I was 25 years old and clearly not mature enough to understand the magnitude of all the things involved in abusive relationships. Yet, at that moment, I knew that THIS HAD TO STOP! I kept thinking, "How could we raise our baby in this environment? How awful would it be for her to think that this behavior was acceptable?" I didn't grow up in this type of living condition so naturally I wanted to protect her from it. After I could take no more of the screams and sounds of someone dragging a kicking body across my ceiling, I went upstairs and knocked on the door with a baseball bat. I literally used the bat to knock on the door. He opened the door and seemed extremely surprised at what appeared before him. I had never seen him or her before, or maybe I had and just didn't know that they lived above me. I looked him in the eyes, and I did not flinch. I was angry. I said in the calmest voice I could muster - and I'm sure he had to listen harder because this voice is usually low and monotone, "Are you the owner of this dwelling?"

He said, "No."

I said, in my low, monotone voice, "Then get me the person who pays the co-op note for this apartment!"

He says something in another language to the woman whom I couldn't see at the time, and once he stopped speaking, she slowly appeared behind him. As she walked toward the door, I can see that she is bloodied and bruised, extremely meek, and afraid. I became infuriated to a level of anger I have never known. I wanted to "bash mister's head in and thank about heaven later" (like in *The Color Purple*) even though I knew that I was pregnant, and I knew this man was violent. I was also painfully aware that I couldn't save her from her own hell and that calling the police would change nothing (I'd called them the last two times this happened). However, I also knew that I COULD NOT LIVE LIKE THIS!

I said to her, "My name is Tommalisa, and I live in the apartment below you. I have decided that TODAY is the last fucking day that I will live with the constant beating, screaming, and dragging. I want you to know that I have no problem helping you beat this man bloody, but I'm about to have a baby right now, and I'm in no position to fight. I want you to know that my next step from here will be a written letter to the homeowners' association to have you removed from this location as I am sure I'm not the only one who can hear what is happening here." I turned and left. I don't know what changed, but he never beat her again during the time we lived beneath them. After our encounter, I saw him only once in the corner neighborhood grocery store a couple of months after Kelsie was born. He was peeking at me between two floor displays in the grocery store. I looked him in the eye because I wanted him to know I saw him, but I said nothing and kept going.

Some will say that I shouldn't have gone upstairs to confront them and that may all be true, but fear, anger, and prenatal hormones (coupled with a mean streak) drove me to it. My Dad taught us a long time ago that men who abuse women are weak and have low self-esteem. Dad taught us to always stand up for ourselves, and to never let a man control us. LaTonya and I knew that he would always protect us. This made all the difference in the world. I remember the day my first husband asked my Dad if he could marry me. I listened undetected by the door and heard my Dad say, "Marriage is hard and requires work from the both of you. I will trust you with my daughter, but if you ever feel the need to put your hands on her, I advise you to call me first because if you hurt her, I will do the jail time." God, I love my Daddy, and he was right to prepare us for this all-too-common phenomenon. "One in four women, and 1 in 7 men, will experience relationship violence in their lives. From 2003–2012, domestic violence accounted for nearly a quarter of all violent victimizations[vi]."

No one plans to be a victim, but everyone should have their guards up and be aware of the tell-tale signs. "While no one type of man abuses women, in studies abusive men share certain characteristics. A Harvard University study showed convicted physically abusive men were found to, when compared to the average American man, commit more crimes as well as:

Have lower levels of education and IQ;
Be less clear-thinking;
Be more neurotic, anxious, nervous and defensive;
Be less agreeable, optimistic, content and more irritable;
Be less extraverted, conscientious and open;
Be less self-confident;
Be more excitable, moody, hasty, and self-centered,
Be more authoritarian.

These characteristics of men who abuse women alone show that they are more likely to lash out when provoked. Some men even show pride in abusing women. Commented the author of the Harvard study: "Instead of being ashamed, they seemed proud when they talked about kicking, biting, or slapping their wives and girlfriends 20 or more times in the past year[vii]." I couldn't take it anymore, and I didn't want my daughter to think any of what was going on with us or around us was normal or healthy, so I made the decision to leave.

Divorce is no respecter of children. It is an ugly disease that spreads through a family leaving hideous scars. I will never be able to understand how two people could be filled with so much love on the front end of a marriage, and the extreme opposite on the back end of a divorce. Husbands and wives literally move from "filled with love" to "filled with loathing" before they even know what has hit them. It just baffles me even though I was one of them. I remember several years after my divorce was final, I swore I would never get married again. I had a really unhealthy perspective on marriage and took it out on every man I met. During that time, my daughter loved Disney princess movies. While watching the ending of *The Little Mermaid* with Kel and my mom one day, I looked at my Mom and said, "I'll give Ariel one good year before she's calling her dad asking for her damn fin back!"

According to Andrew Cherlin, author of *Marriage, Divorce, and Remarriage*, children of parents who go through multiple divorces make lower grades than their peers and are thought of as "less pleasant to be around." Additionally, teenagers who grow up in single-parent or blended families are 300% more likely to require psychological help than their peers. Shockingly, children from divorced families also have more psychological scars **than those who lost a parent to death.** Although Kelsie's Dad and I had our differences, I never wanted her to experience the pain or consequences of our breakup. I believe that divorce is a silent assassin of a child's self-esteem, sense of security, hopes, and dreams. Tread lightly through these emotional years. The children are the most important focus. Tighten your seatbelt because this ride will be turbulent, and there is no way to anticipate the weather patterns...or should I say **emotional** patterns. Everyone involved will be affected.

Divorce was one of the most painful experiences of my life. I packed up my three-year-old daughter, moved her from Queens, New York to Knoxville, Tennessee. I had just gotten accepted to the MBA program at the University of Tennessee at Knoxville and was very fortunate that my parents didn't hesitate to step in to help me with my daughter while I completed the two-year program requirements. The absence of balance was a constant during those days. After the separation, I had to plan for a life of single parenting and grad school made the most sense as the next best step. There was a lot of pressure leaving my daughter with my parents while I was off at school. Not only did I contend with impeding on my parents' and sister's lives, but how hard must it have been on a little girl to be separated from her dad and only seeing her mom during the holidays, school breaks, and summertime. I often think back on this time in my life with great pain for my daughter. You don't ever see the danger when you are sitting in the eye of the storm. At the time, I didn't consider the effect divorce would have on my little girl even though all the statistics were there. Divorce makes for insecure kids who contend internally with their world crumbling all around them. I will never forget the anguish I felt for tearing her world apart, yet I could not shake the haunting thoughts of who she'd become if I had exposed her to a life of two parents that argued 90% of the time. I knew that life could be better for Kelsie.

I learned in my first marriage that being happily married takes hard work. When the marriage suffers, and the parents argue, the children suffer the most. I felt it important that little Kelsie understood that the breakup between her dad and me had nothing to do with how we felt about her, and that we did not get divorced because of her. It would take several more years before any of us could move forward with our lives. Kelsie's dad and I had our differences, but I knew that her father's presence in her life was key. I believe there is something in that chemistry that should not be tampered with. Kids need love and validation from both parents.

I've learned that it's best to be open and transparent as much as you can with everyone you can when going through a divorce. Focus on building some super memories with the people along your journey that make life worth living. Learn to say ABSOLUTELY NOT *and mean it* to protect your family time with your kids. Remind your kids how much you love them and reinforce that they have nothing to do with why you are getting a divorce. They are also suffering during this time, and no matter how much code you use in conversations with others about your divorce, kids know exactly what you are saying. You can still guide them in the right direction while helping them see that greatness is achievable despite the hardship of divorce.

I didn't grow up in a "Cliff and Clair Huxtable" home, as my husband always called my family, but my Mom and Dad are still married today and have been a positive example of a good marriage. I needed Kelsie to know that a relationship between two people could be happy. Shame on the two of us for not being mature enough to provide that example for her. Two years later, with my MBA in hand and a new sales position with Eli Lilly, Kel and I set out on a new and exciting journey. I purchased my first home and tried my best to make a better life for my beautiful, young daughter. I remember the day we moved into our house. Oh, how I cried! I cried tears of joy, tears for many years of pain, embarrassment, fear, self-doubt, for Kel, for my parents, for every pain-staking moment that led us there, and I was grateful and proud. I was every emotion you could imagine, and for the first time in a long time, I had hope for a brighter future for both of us.

7.

Harnessing Their Superpowers

March 24, 2018

Lex: "Mom, how did you know that I was gonna' do something big in my life?"

Me: "What do you mean, honey?"

Lex: "When I was little, you would always say that I was destined for greatness...how did you know that already?"

Me: "Moms are given special insight."

Kids become the highest version of themselves when we believe in their dreams also.

April 22, 2017

Lex: Sometimes, the only fun I have at school is at recess, and when I'm sitting across from the girl I have a crush on at lunch.

Me (initial thought in my head): Wait, what the hell did he just say? (Praying out loud on purpose so he can hear) "Jesus, Lord, have mercy! Please keep my sweet lil' fella' away from girls until the age of about 65. Please make him see that girls are nothin' but trouble and strife and will reap havoc on his life. In the name of Jesus, I pray, amen."

Lex: "Lord, please tell my mom that girls are not that bad and make her let me have a girlfriend BEFORE I am an old man....and Lord was my momma' trouble when my dad met her? Please show me a sign. In the name of Jesus, I pray, amen!"

Me: 😳 😣

#icantstandlex! #damnkidsgonekillme #lordpleasegivemesomebettercomebacks

Lawd, have mercy!

~ ~ ~

How do you pull everything your kid is capable of out of him or her? I mean *everything* - everything they want to give and everything they have to give but often don't give. How do you get beyond "surviving parenting" to "thriving parenting?" Every single child is born with a special gift, and I believe it is our job as parents to watch, learn, and identify these talents to give our kids everything they need to be successful. My husband and I made a pact when the boys were infants that we would be intentional in raising them - intentional about guiding them, intentional about who and what they were exposed to, and intentional about their training. We decided that we would not put "old school" (i.e. children are to be seen and not heard) boundaries on them and that we would try to expose them to as many opportunities as we could, where it made sense, of course. Our goal was to identify and to help them develop and understand their God-given strengths.

Now herein lies the challenge. We had no way to know - while changing diapers or bottle-feeding them - if they would be the next Mozart or Nobel Peace Prize winner or not, but we knew that we wanted to help them reach their purpose in life. We would be vigilant and disciplined in mapping out a plan to build a solid foundation beneath them. T was the cornerstone for finding opportunities, and I would put the opportunity to action. This was our late-night pillow talk, still is, and there is nothing sexy about it. We talk a lot about what we think the boys are good at, have a passion for, and what we think might be the logical next steps to put in place for them to succeed. We also welcome advice from others where it makes sense. There is nothing new under the sun. Why should we try to recreate the wheel?

Three pieces of advice that made a great deal of difference for the boys came from my parents and two good friends. The first was Purdue Jr. Vet Camp. A good friend I'll call KB told us about this camp for kids which exposed them to careers in veterinary medicine. The second was information about the Indianapolis Repertory Theatre from a second friend, HBS, who told us that her daughter had been in productions there and enjoyed it. The third was when my mom taught us how to get the boys accustomed to doing homework when they were just two and three years old. She instructed us to sit them down every day after school – starting at that young age - and give them a blank sheet of paper and crayons, modeling clay, or finger paints (anything really) for a few minutes. She said that this would teach them early to sit down right after school and do their homework. It worked like a charm! Both boys, as soon as they get home from school, do their homework without being told.

We also try hard as parents to give the boys room to explore. TJ has an amazing ability to draw and a scientific interest in nature. Lex has an uncanny ability to create captivating stories and movies on his own. We would not have known of TJ's interests and artistic abilities if we had not purchased an easel, nor Lex's ability to make stop motion movies if we hadn't allowed him to use our cell phone from time to time when he'd ask us. TJ was ten years old when he drew the pictures below. As you can see, he also loves animals.

TiJuan Jr. (10)

TJ's love for animals became clear to us when he was about six years old, and we watched his passion grow and develop. I remember one year that we had a chipmunk epidemic in our neighborhood. They were everywhere and dug holes all over the yard. T wanted to find a way to get rid of them permanently, and TJ begged his dad to let him catch them in his small cage and release them somewhere away from the house in the woods. Believe it or not, that is exactly what we did! TJ caught a chipmunk every week all summer long. It was scary for me to put the cage in our car, but we did it! The release became fun for me! The excitement of watching the chipmunks run into the trees with the boys running after them trying to keep up was hilarious. The thing I loved most was watching TJ research what chipmunks like to eat (to know what to put in his cage to lure them) and watching him keep a log of the different foods he offered them to see which one worked best. TJ got so good at it that he helped other families get rid of their chipmunk infestations. I was in total learning mode watching his dedication.

I still remember when TJ caught his first frog in the front yard and begged us to let him keep it. It was disgusting to me. The little monster's wet and slimy skin and huge mouth were unnerving, and there was something vulgar about the way it ate worms. Now I know that's the way it was intended to be but were we really intended to cohabitate with it? Absolutely not - but try telling six-year-old TJ that. Ugh! I was always in a state of panic around TJ because he would constantly catch me off guard with all the bugs, snakes, frogs and critters he'd find all over the yard and in the woods behind our home. When he caught his first frog, I tried to explain that creatures in the wild don't want to be caged. They like to live freely. He heard "they like to live," and that was it. T and I both agreed to let him keep it for one week, and he would have to let the frog go. TJ caught worms and crickets for the lil' guy, and let him go after one week. One day shortly after the release of his first frog, he came home from school full of excitement. He said his teacher had asked him to catch a frog for the class and she would allow TJ to take care of it. We learned from this experience that TJ was responsible and considerate and could be trusted to take good care of his animals. TJ was diligent in taking care of the class pet frog. He would dig up worms and take them to school, change the water in the aquarium and mist the frog regularly with a spray bottle filled with water. When he got older, he would spend his allowance at the pet store. He'd buy aquariums, soil and anything he could find to take care of whatever he could catch. He also loves to go fishing and camping. We would, on occasion, allow him to go fishing in the neighborhood ponds. Although we try to give him these freedoms sometimes, he gets caught being 14.

One day I went up to his room and discovered that TJ had captured four wild fish and put them in one of the aquariums he'd purchased from the pet store. Imagine my surprise when I walked in on him feeding crickets to these wild fish! This was extremely stressful for me because I could never be sure of what he might find and whether it would be poisonous or not. He was also notorious for finding dead things and bringing them home to me to ask if he could cut it open to see how they looked on the inside. The first dead animal he found was an old decaying snake. TJ was only about five or six years old when this happened. Another time he somehow found a bird full of maggots. Yes, it's tough to let children have such freedom to grow and explore and, of course, we threw both of those dead animals away, but we immediately started buying animal books. TJ asked for his first medical encyclopedia for animals when he was 11. Through the years, his love for animals and genuine desire to take care of them evolved. We began to look for ways to cultivate his love for animals and by the time TJ got to 7th grade, he was selected to attend Purdue University's Jr. Vet Camp for one week. He had to apply and write an essay and we all were excited for him when he got accepted. TJ is now 14 and is still interested in becoming a veterinarian when he gets older.

TiJuan Jr. (13) at Purdue's Jr. Veterinarian Camp. Summer 2018.

There were other things we did to help develop the boys when they were younger. We kept them busy with activities like arts and crafts and writing short stories. I would also make up games to keep them in a thinking mode. One of my favorite games was *"Then What Happened."* This was a game I made up one day out of desperation to keep them entertained while we were at a car dealership looking at trucks. It's a fun game where someone starts telling a story and, to move the story along, you must point to the next person and say, "then what happened?" The selected player then must add to the story where the last person left off. Of course, the stories got crazy at times, but we enjoyed a lot of funny moments together, and it helped the boys to think creatively and quickly while building on the story. We had lots of fun with all sorts of games and activities – we even made a robot together along with a pet robot dog.

TJ (5), Robot, and Lex (4)

Every child is different, and we soon discovered that Lex had unique interests growing up as well. While he was never interested in animals like TJ, Lex was always finding ways to make everyone laugh. Now making people laugh wasn't necessarily what I considered a superpower per se, but this kid definitely had passion for it. I remember the days when I'd pull up to the summer camp at Eli Lilly (where I worked at the time) to pick up the boys, and on several occasions, I'd find Lex in the middle of the camp counselors making them laugh. I don't know what he'd be saying, but it had to be funny. I observed this same behavior when both boys would play with the neighborhood kids. One day as T and I were walking over to the neighbor's home to chat a bit and to pick the boys up, there was Lex in the middle of the parents (not the kids), and they were cracking up. T and I looked at each other, and one of us said, "Lord, what in the world is he over there saying to the neighbors? How can a kid so young have so much funny stuff to say?" Here's a nugget of wisdom I can absolutely share from my years of parenting - even if your kid displays unconventional abilities or shows a strong interest in areas you know nothing about, take notice and watch. It could very well turn into something you could never imagine in your wildest dreams. The day Lex asked me to put him in a movie or a commercial, I laughed it off and told him it didn't work quite that way. Little did we know just how serious he was about acting.

With Lex, it seemed his brain was way more mature than his numerical age. He was quick with wit and always seemed to gravitate to writing stories and making up songs and beat-boxing. He even made movies with his Legos. To make "stop motion" videos he would painstakingly move the Lego pieces and shoot one frame after every move he made and then piece the frames together to make a movie. He would add his own special effects and narrate the movie as well. It was amazing to watch him do this, and I remember most of his elementary years I was constantly asking him, "Did you do that by yourself?" or "How did you know how to do that?" I remember being impressed with his movies and stories and marveled at his ability to make quality storylines. He also made a Nerf movie short and added TJ. It was filled with action-packed scenes and rapid shooting and the dodging of nerf bullets. Lex always liked to write scenes and then drive us all crazy acting out the parts. Lex was always thinking of ways to bring his storylines and creative characters to life. He started asking T a lot about starting a YouTube channel, but we were not comfortable with its safety at the time and the work involved in Lex keeping the channel going over time. Vloggers put a lot of time and effort into what they do, and we just didn't want him to get too overwhelmed with the upkeep at such a young age.

Lex started doing his characters around the house, and he was hilarious! He asked me to help him with the makeup and costumes, and when T and I saw how serious and committed he was T started an Instagram account for Lex's first character, Uncle Velvet. He would go on to create other characters, several actually, that were as entertaining as they were funny. He created Lil' Breezy, Louis Obama (President Obama's lesser-known brother), and more. He even started doing impressions and we just sat back and watched this kid take off like a rocket. He could impersonate Will Smith, Kevin Hart, Chris Rock, Eddie Murphy, Jason Statham, President Obama, and recently he's been working on Denzel Washington.

Lex (13) 2019 Kids Choice Awards

Setting boundaries is an integral part of our role as parents with TJ and Lex. We guard against activities that sponge their time and don't add value. It's a hard task to pull ourselves away from the devices, let alone our boys! When the boys commit to an activity or a goal, we are adamant that they complete it. Lex was also frustrated at times because we would make him wait until he was TJ's age to have privileges that TJ got to have first because he was older (like getting a cell phone or an Instagram account). I'll never forget the day that T discovered that Lex had an "unapproved" (unbeknownst to us), Instagram account. He had it for a month before we ever knew about it. Lex was always the one to break T's codes on restricted accounts. It got to be quite comical for me to watch T, Director of IT, looking to see what code Lex might break next. That kid was unbelievable and hard to keep contained. Lex was always quick at most things and extremely smart. It's safe to say that Lex was like an old soul who'd been here before. I can't tell you the number of close friends who have said that to us throughout the years. Mom and Dad picked up on it years ago when Lex was very young.

There are also developmental areas that are non-negotiables for us like learning to play the piano. T signed the boys up to play the piano at the YMCA when TJ was five years old. Lex had to wait because he was too young or at least that's what they told us at the Y. Shortly after TJ started playing, my husband found a piano coach who would not only come to our home to teach them but also let Lex start at the age of four. The non-negotiable is that the boys will continue to play the piano until they leave for college and hopefully, will continue to play beyond their high school years. We also tried to find ways for the boys to use their talents in ways that would give back to the community. T and I decided one day that the boys needed to volunteer to learn humility and develop a "give back" mentality. I stopped by an Assisted Living facility one day to see if they had a piano and to inquire about their volunteer program. I cannot tell you how key it is to create opportunities for your kids. I simply went in, asked for the activities coordinator and showed her a short clip of each of the boys playing the piano. As a result, TJ and Lex have been playing for that Assisted Living Facility twice a year for three consecutive years. Each year in the spring and fall they select four to five songs each, create a postcard-sized program to highlight the songs they will play and run the whole program on their own. One opens the program, and the other closes it. T and I sit and watch the show in the audience. We purposely allowed them to do it on their own as we feel that it is a great opportunity for the boys to give back, learn how to present to a large audience, and build confidence. At least 80% of their preschool and elementary school years were filled with opportunities for them to think outside the box and use their creativity to explore opportunities. These were great developmental times for the boys, and T and I had fun watching them grow.

Managing Instagram and the other social media accounts our teens seem tethered to has been particularly challenging while working through the puberty years. They can't get great at anything when they are always playing a video game. It is frustrating to consistently have to prod, probe, push, and fuss with these teens, especially when we no longer recognize or understand them. It's a new way of living that frazzles my nerves. The more they try to assert their independence, the more they experiment and test their boundaries. Lord, how I miss nap time and tiny feet running around our home! It becomes more difficult during the puberty years to convince them of the importance of perfecting their talents and skills. Somehow super talents aren't super important to them.

Constant teen rebellion makes it difficult for a parent not to throw in the towel and ignore them. Video games give rise to the most rebellious moments in our home and are one of the biggest superpower killers (my opinion). The boys got so engrossed in the games at one point that T had to enact a moratorium on video games for six months. Now, mind you, this moratorium became a punishment for me too. Why? Because now I had to enforce a law that I didn't make or agree with and, don't tell my husband, but I felt that six months was too long for any kid to endure. However, I would never disagree with hubby once the gavel was struck. Divisive parenting is not our style. However, I do have my weak moments.

Lex and I had to travel to LA for seven weeks during episodic season, and while there I broke down and let him play. I felt like he should be rewarded for all his hard work. I could not have been more wrong. The one-time "pass" turned into every chance he got. Lex even tried to play video games while I was getting dressed one morning instead of going over his lines and prepping for an audition we were headed to. When I noticed it, I told him that "there is a time for working hard and a time for play, and right now it is time for working hard." I got dressed, cooked him breakfast, and told him to run through his lines while I ate. It was painfully clear that playing video games was more important than locking in his lines. He became short with me when I tried to tell him that this behavior would not be tolerated. He then tried to "Jedi Mind Trick" me by telling me that I hadn't seen what I'd just seen, which was him being upset with me for making him delete Fortnite from his iPad.

It was then that I had to admit that my moments of weakness can hurt them more than I thought. Dare I say it? T's moratorium was the right decision to make. The boys are a lot more productive, their attitudes are more positive, and they spend more time on constructive projects when they are not playing video games. Being a good parent, the type of parent that will lean in to make them the best person they can be, is hard. I sometimes want to throw my body to the floor and kick and scream at the top of my lungs, "I don't want to be an adult today!" This, however, was one of those times when I realized that digging deep was imperative. Until our teens become adults, our job is not yet complete.

I believe that your outlook on life as a parent is developed from childhood. My parenting style with my kids evolved from the environment in which I grew up. Tommy and Effie Alexander were very supportive parents. They would push us to be the best at whatever we endeavored and, as far as identifying my "super talents," well, I think they showed up as a result of being bullied in school. I am not afraid of the elephant in the room. I excelled in my role in HR as a result of my childhood learnings. My parents were sticklers for accountability, self-awareness, honesty, and integrity. My dad would always ask me, "Why do you care what people say about you? Don't you know who you are? You are enough standing alone by yourself. It doesn't matter what others think about you. It's what you think about yourself that is key." Mom would remind me of the old adage often, "Your attitude determines your altitude in life." She would also say, "Things will happen, and not all of it will be positive, but it is up to you to determine how you will deal with it." This was their way of equipping me to deal with bullying growing up. In retrospect, their advice helped me to overcome the hardships I faced at school.

I was teased a lot. I have a huge, black birthmark on my left thigh. As a young girl growing up in the '70s and '80s with a birthmark that size - the kids were brutal. There were no anti-bullying policies then - you sucked it up and dealt with it. They would say things like, "Here, Spot! Here, Spot (whistling as one would to call a dog)!" They would also call me names like "blackie," "soot," or "Black Sambo."" I remember coming home often burdened with sadness, and my parents would always give me words of encouragement. They would also make sure that I understood that when people said mean things about me it was their way of hiding the fact that they were not happy with themselves. What others said about me simply did not matter. My mom had great experience handling these types of situations and was brilliant in how she shaped our minds. I teach a very similar mindset with the boys. I will allow them moments to be down, but when it's time to snap out of it, I say, "Let's start looking for solutions. How are we going to deal with this situation?" I always tell them that it's okay to make mistakes - it's all in how you make the situation "right."

Menopause has also taught me grace and wisdom. I have moments of clarity betwixt and between moments of rage, sadness, and frustration. It is during the moments of clarity that I've learned to be ok in silence. Fussing became the knee jerk answer to everything when I entered menopause and it's exhausting. I lean on one particular scripture a lot of late. "Be still and know that I am God." (Psalm 46:10) Have you come across a mirror during one of your fussing rants? Oh, it ain't pretty, and I almost burst into laughter the first time it happened by accident. Veins were popping out everywhere, there were wrinkles on my forehead and around my eyes, and no one was really listening because I fuss "all of the time." The only thing missing was fire flaming from my nostrils. Eventually, I learned that I got more mileage when I was quiet, stared, or ignored the behavior. Sometimes life lessons, if the consequences are minimal, are the best teachers. As I've gotten older, I've gotten better at silence and watching. This is my new normal.

T and I believe in pushing the boys beyond their comfort zones. That's how we learned just how capable they were. We are firm when it's required, and we have fun with them sometimes also. We try to build in a healthy amount of balance and often check in with them to get a gage for their level of self-awareness. We don't ever allow them to give up, and once they start something, we do not let them quit. They don't have to sign up for it again if they don't like the sport or activity, but they will not quit, and they will replace the activity with something else. No matter what happens, we don't allow them to be mediocre or what some call "half-assed." They both must give 100% effort to what they are doing - if not, why are they wasting their time? Every child needs to be pushed beyond their comfort zones. If they are never pushed, they will never know their true potential for greatness!

I sometimes think of Joe Jackson or Lavar Ball - am I that bad? Lex would say yes. I don't think so. I just feel that when kids don't want to do it and you press in hard, you are really helping them. I don't beat them, but I believe if you can play video games for an hour, you can read for an hour. T made up the rule that there is a timer - however long you play video games, that's how long you must play the piano or read a book. Get a timer to gauge how long. Now the frustrations are turned to the timer.

As you look in your young ones in the eyes and watch where their greatest passion lies, you can begin to push them in the direction of their greatness. My mom calls this "Hook-ups from Heaven." Look for every opportunity possible to help them develop master-level skills. Harness their superpowers and help your kids use them for good and whatever you do, don't let them give up on their dreams. I often think of a quote from the movie *The Last Samurai,* which inspired me, "From the moment they wake they devote themselves to the perfection of whatever they pursue." I have never seen such discipline. The Japanese warrior, in the movie, devoted himself totally to a moral code of discipline to master the sword and to train his mind to seek stillness. This commitment to perfection had a lasting impression on me.

I must admit, however, with all of our "pressing in" and pushing the boys to commit to their personal best, there is a part of me that continues to check in on them. Are they happy? Is this the best approach for the boys? How do you help your kids strive to be the best they can be while balancing their happiness and keeping them whole? That's where my heart is torn at times.

During this season of acting, Lex can't play football. It breaks my heart. He loves it. Watching Lex see his team at practice his first season out was torture for T and I. We questioned our decision to allow him to go to LA for seven weeks to pursue acting and really dealt with the question, "Are we doing the right thing?" We had to "dig deep" and make some tough decisions for both boys. They are constant and challenging decisions with no definite insight on outcomes. All we know is that once the decision is made, we are all committed to it. Making the decision to homeschool Lex was a tough one. He was still enrolled in school while we were in LA for seven weeks during the fall of 2018 and he was expected to do all the work his classmates were doing while attending acting classes in the evenings. It was challenging to manage this schedule, and Lex was getting the bulk of the hit. Homeschooling was absolutely the right answer if he was to be successful in this new pursuit of acting.

The approach to unraveling the mystery of your kid's superpower has no direct path or pattern. You will know it when you see it, and even when you discover what it is, just know that there is a load of work, decisions, and sacrifices ahead to help them be successful. You will sometimes experience rebellion and push back from your teen and you will have to sometimes show them where they are headed to keep them focused. Some kids are totally dedicated and will drag you to where they are headed. They are all different. You will have to "press in" as a parent, do your research and allow them to try.

8.

Dig Deep

April 12, 2015

I rode my bike with some friends today, and I was exhausted by the time we returned. When I got home, I found TJ and Lex waiting for me with their bikes already out of the garage ready to ride.

TJ and Lex, overlapping each other: "There you are! We've been waiting for you! Will you ride with us? We are gonna' stay in the neighborhood, we promise….What took you so long?.....If we see a frog can I keep it?"

Me, with tears in my eyes and a numb ass, thighs, calves, hams, and traps (I literally had dried up salt on my face from the sweat): "Please boys, I'm exhausted…I just road 23 miles…I don't have anything left to give, for the love of God and all that is holy don't make me hate you both!"

TJ: "Man up! Those are just excuses, and nobody wants to hear 'em!"

Lex, shaking his head: "Excuses are tools of…!" (Some crap that T usually says to them. I stopped listening.)

Begrudgingly, I drug my lifeless body back on my bike and threatened them both within an inch of their lives if they tried to ride farther than our neighborhood boundaries. I secretly held a grudge against them both for taking THIS moment to use our (mine and T's) words against me?!

Yeah, not my best mommy moment.
This was parenting backlash and it sucked.

Being a 54-year-old mom of 12 and 13-year-old-boys has its challenges.

~~~

Shapeshifting parents know how to dig deep. I have learned to master it. A few of my shape-shifting attributes include morphing into an actress, party planner, decorator, balloon-inflator, and party-game builder. Other roles include set director, light holder, prop builder, set designer, camerawoman, and costume department for Lex's Uncle Velvet skits and other productions. I've also been known to shift into an Uber driver, a lunatic, an assistant veterinarian, cricket and mealworm fetcher, baby mice picker-upper and "momager" to name just a few more. It all depends on the circumstances we're facing as a family that day. How many times have you contorted yourself to be whatever your family needed at the time? I'll wait…exactly! Probably too many to count!

Digging deep can mean different things in different situations from going the extra mile for our teens because they are deserving of the best we can give them, to locking yourself in your bedroom just to watch a movie in peace to keep from going upside puberty's head. Most parents are no stranger to making sacrifices for their kids. When I speak of "digging deep," I imagine it's a concept many parents can relate to.

"Digging Deep" is what I call giving everything you have to give, going at least four steps farther when thinking through an idea, or pushing yourself and others to achieve an outcome you never imagined reaching. "Digging Deep" requires that you push past hunger, fatigue, and personal needs and desires to accomplish your ultimate goals for your family. It can also mean controlling your "I'm about to snap on you if you don't stop calling my name over and over, emotions!" You either decide to "dig deep" or you are forced to do it. I have yet to find my limits, and I venture to say that there can be no limits to pushing yourself and your kids farther than either of you ever thought possible. I am guilty of going way beyond what's required to get the best possible results.

One example was the time the boys wanted to wear bow ties for a special event (it was also fashionable to wear them to school on game days (they had to "dress up" on game day)). Of course, it was last minute, so I ran immediately into the pantry and transformed into a "bow tie maker." With the help of a DIY video, I became proficient at making bow ties. Have you seen the price tag on men's bow ties lately? Unreal! I made several in many different colors with matching handkerchiefs. It's not an easy task, but boy is it rewarding. I choose to dig deep to make the bow ties "happen" for TJ and Lex.

"Digging Deep" requires tapping into your inner perfectionist. I read an article once about understanding the power of a great headline. The basic premise was that eight out of ten people will read a headline, but only two out of that ten will actually read the article. They suggest that the writer write 25 headlines for each piece of content to gain the strongest headline to grow readership. I know this relates to a different subject matter, but it has the same premise. Will you be that 25-headline parent? I'm the parent who will write 50 headlines to be sure I have enough. *Going several steps further to get to the greatest outcome is ingrained in me.*

I will typically take an existing thought like planning a birthday party for the kids and come up with ways to make it better than they could have ever imagined. Here again, I made the *choice* to dig deep. Birthday parties are big deals to me. I think it stems from my childhood days. My mom and dad were known for having some great parties for us growing up. I remember the flashlight party they hosted for me where they had flashlights for all the kids. It was awesome. When the song *Flashlight* by Parliament started playing, we lost our minds! Then there was my

Sweet Sixteen Surprise Party. I remember feeling so happy and so loved.

I think that's what I want the boys to feel when we plan parties for them or when we push them to give 150% effort in whatever they do. The outcome is always better than they could imagine, and that feeling of accomplishment and pride is priceless. I go way beyond what's necessary when I plan their parties and I push the boys to do the same with ideas that they may have with almost anything they think of doing. Needless to say, we've had some awesome birthday parties with the boys. One favorite was TJ's pirate party where we all dressed as pirates and T made the "laddies" walk the plank. I made a mast and sail out of the party table and ordered cupcakes with black icing on them. Each kid had to have a sash, an eye patch, a sword, and a headscarf. I soaked paper in tea water several days in advance to give it time to dry and then burned the edges to get an authentic look to the signs and flyers. It was an awesome party!

Lex (6) and TJ (8) at TJ's 8th Birthday Party

TJ's 8th Birthday Pirate Party

Our Family Dressed Like the Bob's Burgers Crew

"Digging Deep" requires pushing past your extreme desire to rest or the pain of those menopausal joints to complete strenuous tasks with or for puberty. I remember during episodic season in LA with Lex, I'd just settled in from a long day of what felt like perpetual perilous driving and Lex just wouldn't stop talking. Like in the biking scenario in the opening of this chapter, I was tired and eager to be left alone. It was a true menopausal moment where his lips were moving, but I was already on a beach far away somewhere on a sailboat drinking margaritas and riding the tide. It was warm and beautiful, and I could hear the whales in the distance. What a peaceful, pleasant thought until Lex pulled me back to reality.

Lex: "Mom, are you listening?"

Me: "Of course

I am."

I even repeated what he'd just said back to him. I just did not want to engage, and I certainly did not want to talk about building a Lego Jurassic World. I struggle with trying to be a good mom and knowing when to shut down and have some "me" time. It is in these moments, and many others like it, where I ask myself if I should "dig deeper" and build memories with my son or protect my temperament because I will surely snap if I don't protect my sanity. Finally, in Lex's mantra of monologued conversation, I hear, "Mom, don't make me judge you!"

I thought, "Judge away, lil' boy, because duct tape on your mouth might turn you against me for life!" He was talking nonstop, and I needed him to stop. Of course, that was only a conversation in my head. Thank goodness he can't read or hear my thoughts. I did not work on building Jurassic World on this night, but I grabbed him up and gave him a big hug and kiss and I told him how much I loved him. I did, however, rearrange the dinosaurs every couple of days to his surprise and excitement. Some days the dinosaurs were eating the people in his makeshift village or stepping on them to get to a nearby truck or tree. Lex seemed to get a kick out of this. I believe that moms are made of special resiliency cells. We would bend the moon and realign the stars for our kids even when we don't feel like it. "Digging Deep" in this instance required me to push past my comfort zone and position Lex's dinosaurs to engage in something that Lex enjoyed doing.

There are times when I'm on the beach in my mind, but when it's stormy, aka "Lumpkin Boy Shenanigan Time," I'm never ready for it when it hits. I find myself juggling between several thoughts and emotions, and by the time the waves come crashing in around me, I'm already underwater. "Digging Deep" is simply not drowning at that moment. My ability to handle the floodgate of emotions in a timely manner has failed me on many occasions. Most of the time, I'm just trying to stay afloat. Often in settling a dispute between the boys, I don't have a choice. I must muster the strength to be firm with them. I'm basically in grandma years (the age where you should be spoiling the grandkids and giving them back to their parents) trying to raise puberty. Menopausal parents of puberty don't have that luxury.

Both TJ and Lex are busy with extracurriculars. They both have been somewhat successful in the activities they've ventured to try. It requires a lot of motivation and sacrifice from all of us. T and I spend many moments thinking through how to continue to motivate TJ and Lex. We don't mind making the sacrifices, and we continue to encourage them. Just this year, for example, we put our home on the market to sell and are moving to LA to give Lex a chance with acting. T has also done extensive research to find the best training in LA for high school basketball. TJ not only goes to agility training, but he also goes to a private trainer. While in LA during pilot season with Lex, I worked with an agency to get TJ representation for modeling. These are just a few examples of the sacrifice we are more than willing and happy to make to secure a brighter future for both boys. While in LA they both continue piano lessons and while TJ is at basketball training Lex is taking Taekwondo. We are proud of the boys for all the hours they put into training. If you are currently on the bubble about your son or daughter's current passions and are concerned about how much more to invest in them...just do it! You never know where the next step forward will lead them.

T and I were in that same position just a year ago with Lex. We knew Lex loved acting and at the time had three plays, five national commercials, and a bucket load of auditions behind him. We weren't sure if we should guide this ship forward or drop anchor. One question we pondered for quite some time was how deep were we willing to dig to make this happen? To move forward would require our family to make some major decisions. T and I discussed enrolling him in schools with advanced theatrical curriculums. We had to research where these schools were located and if it was a viable possibility. I reached out to Lex's agent in Indiana and T and I agreed to allow him to travel to LA for a week to participate in a showcase at Gray Studios in North Hollywood. This gave him exposure to LA agents and managers and would ultimately confirm whether this was the right decision to make on Lex's behalf. On June 10th Lex and I flew out to LA for one week. His showcase was Thursday, June 14, 2018. Lex had done such a great job in his performance that he had several agents and management groups interested in interviewing him. By September 13, 2018 Lex had LA representation with Abrams Artist Agency and Crackerjack Management. At the time he also had Midwest representation (Helen Wells Agency in Indianapolis and Hall Talent out of Louisville, KY).

It has indeed been a fun journey with the boys and, given my age, I'm constantly weighing my ability to keep pushing forward on their behalf. I know at this juncture, "digging deep" is not an option. What they are going to need will require everything I have in me. I'm not the rookie on "Team Lumpkin," I feel more like the crypt keeper. I put on the good face of strength, but I'm afraid sometimes. Isn't that crazy?

On some days, I feel like I have it all under control, and sometimes not so much. I've "dug deep" all my life and at some point, there's no more water in the well. When that happens, I start digging a new well. If we were all given one shovel- longevity- my shovel is dull! I have 13- and 14- year-old kids with several years in front of them and I'm working feverishly to build a solid foundation quickly. I won't be defeated, and I won't give up. There is too much at stake. So, when I feel the urge to give in and give up, I push harder and build bolder.

There are two ways to look at it. "Digging Deep" is from a personal position, how do I push the boys to be the best version of themselves? How do I teach them the importance of embracing this concept? In life we have choices - you can choose to do nothing - you can choose to coast through life, or you can choose to be great. Why not strive to be great? We push our boys to strive for greatness. I want them to be confident and love who they are despite this ugly world. I need them to know that they are worthy and capable. That's what "digging deep" means to me and that's why I do it.

Puberty and menopause together require a special set of abilities. Both are dealing with physical, emotional, and cognitive changes, all of which are difficult to process. In addition to puberty's extracurricular activities, they are being pushed academically, mentally, and physically. They know that there are high expectations of them and that they have our support. Parents have a custodial duty ***never to let our guards down.*** We must constantly watch for potential pitfalls and possible no-value-added behaviors that could derail our kid's goals. Parents must also be willing to walk away from opportunities that could prove harmful to our teens despite their protests. ***It's a tough lesson for them to learn but being comfortable will never get you anywhere worthwhile.***

T'Lisa's Tips for Digging Deep

My two sons are polar opposites. They both require different parenting skills from me, and I'm exhausted and unequipped! As a parent, I often feel inadequate because I DON'T KNOW THE ANSWERS! I'm literally "building this plane in flight" (stole that saying from work). The worst is that sometimes I'm too tired to look for parts to build the plane. Parenting is not for the faint of heart. It took me 28 years to learn this, and the learning continues.

In the past, I've broad-brushed my ideas and opinions on my kids because it was easy and required little effort. My (now adult) daughter was raised in a single-parent home when I was young and clueless (forgive me, Kel). I, for the longest, tried to push my "way" and my "agenda" on my kids. Experience has taught me that:

1. Young people are the absolute better versions of us! They come packaged with a whole host of great things that we have never seen before! Let them try sports, music, gymnastics, dance, nature exploration, hair color, etc. and get out of their way. Our job is to set them up for success!

2. Always speak life into their dreams! Be their biggest fans! I firmly believe that our children become who we tell them they are. So, years ago when the boys were very young (at the age of a million questions), I'd say things like, "You can't blend in when you were born to stand out. You were destined for greatness." I'd remind them, "You will soar with the eagles and not gobble with the turkeys." Then I'd ask them, "Why?" I'd even answer for them, "Because eagles fly, and turkeys get eaten! WHICH ONE WILL YOU BE?" And whenever my boys would say they couldn't do something, I would make them recite these words, "There is nothing in the world that I cannot do with the help of Jesus." I have not heard either boy say, "I can't" in years. Lol!

3. Pray for your kids! I don't know who my children will be when they become adults, but I pray that they will be great contributors to society. We hope that we've taught them to make good decisions and to be strong enough to push past the obstacles they will face in life.

4. They must make mistakes in order to learn! T and I tell them firmly when they are wrong and teach them to ALWAYS make it right! This is an absolute must in our home. I love it when they can learn from a really bad situation. My boys get caught being 13 and 14 quite often. We teach them that "mistakes happen in life, but that's not the big deal. The big deal is all in how you make it right! Now, how are you going to make this right?" My kids drive me crazy at times, but I have successfully adjusted my expectations of them! They need space to be who they are and not who I want them to be. I try hard to get out of their way and see what happens.

5. Don't try to parent every child the same. I have to parent Lex, TJ, and Kelsie differently. Lex is very stubborn and responds to mature conversation. You can't pull the wool over his eyes. You have to "give it to him straight" because he's so smart he will see through it if you don't. With TJ, it's more attention and repetition. I sit next to him, and we both face the same way when we talk. He's shy, and I find myself focusing more on the situation and how he feels and what he thinks about it. Lex is more of a face to face person. No, you can't be friends with your children, but you need to take the time to learn their personalities. "One brush stroke parenting" doesn't work. Times change and parenting has to change. Sometimes it seems like being a parent is nature. You make sure they grow and that they're healthy, but if you're trying to teach them values and shape human minds, you will have to **work** as a parent. You must put something valuable in to get something out. This requires you to **get uncomfortable**. Do you think I'm comfortable for 7 weeks in a little apartment, driving all over? No! But I want Lex to be successful, and for him to have these experiences, I have to get uncomfortable. You can't raise your kids to greatness comfortably. When they bitch and moan about practicing the piano, life is uncomfortable, but when they get on stage and play beautifully, they are so proud of themselves. People want to be let off the hook, but it just doesn't work.

6. There is no shortcut. I would challenge moms with this question - how far are you willing to go to make your child the best they can be? If you're not willing to go above and beyond and out of the norm you have to settle that. You must count the cost of what you want for your child. Having a baby in and of itself is uncomfortable. You don't have a choice. It's so easy for them to keep themselves comfortable.

Moms with babies feel it. If there's any way that I can make the outcome different, I will do it. I've always been driven. Whenever I try out for anything, I have to make it. I'll get up at three in the morning and do whatever I have to do to succeed. God gave me three beautiful chances at parenting, and I'm not going to waste them.

7. Allow them to experience life. T is taking TJ to Puerto Rico next week, and the first thing I thought of was my baby somewhere in a tub on ice! If you ever go somewhere and try to come home with just one of my boys, just don't come home. You won't be happy - I don't care what happened. Once, T lost Lex. I was out of town and they went to Monkey Joe's for a birthday party. Lex was probably five and TJ was six. When I'm out of town or away T does other stuff. No one ever told me, but we were watching Criminal Minds and a man came out of the house screaming and crying. T said I know how he feels. I said, "What??? How in the hell do you know how that feels???" He finally confessed. T had lost the boys at Monkey Joe's. The staff bolted the doors and they searched the building. Lex had let himself get talked into going up to the tallest slide and had hid at the top when he was afraid to go down. TJ had gone up and sat with him. When no one could find them, they shut the place down. My husband gives them too much rope. When Lex was six months old, they shared a room. One week I was away on business. When I returned and began cleaning their room, I found poop in random places! WTF??? "T, why is there poop randomly spread around the room?" He

113

had slept in one day when I was gone, and TJ had tried to change Lex's diaper! No one ever told me.

9.

The B Word

July 30, 2013

(TJ, 9 yrs. old)

TJ went to bed a little earlier than usual, and I was sure both boys were down for the night. I'm getting ready for bed when I hear a voice that says, "Hi!" I visit psychiatrists every day as a sales rep, and I hear all kinds of stories about their patients and the voices that speak to them! I was afraid I might be losing my mind. I looked all around the closet, bathroom, and bedroom, but there was no one there. While I'm explaining it to T who is looking at me like he might need to commit me, TJ walks out of our closet through our bedroom and says "goodnight" like nothing happened. I wanted to lay hands on him and not in a "catch the Holy Ghost" way!!

November 11, 2018

Pre-Puberty Logic

Lex: "Mom, TJ ate most of the brownies. He said that he only had two and a half pieces. Now you know he don't eat half of anything (totally irritated)!"

Me: "It's possible to eat half of a piece of something (totally unengaged...I don't really care about this protest)."

Lex: "Mom am I half of a person 'cuz I'm short? No! I'm still a whole person!"

My Thoughts:

- I refuse to be sucked into this conversation, Pre-Puberty, and I'm certainly not going to choose a side!

- Ummm, you are kinda' half the size of a person twice your height. I mean you'd be half a bite if people were food. I'm just sayin'.

- I don't speak "pre-puberty language," and this brownie altercation will be what it will be. I'm tired.

- Why is every situation with you a thing?

July 30, 2015

Lex: "Yo momma so fat she stepped on the scale, and it said, "One at a time please."" #summercampisawaistofourmoney

September 16, 2010

TJ (5) gets a star every day in kindergarten if he brings home all ten of his blessings. He brought home nine today and told Alex (4), "I told myself that I was gonna' be a good listener today. Alex says, "What happened? Didn't you listen to you?" TJ says, "No, but next time I'm gonna' make him listen to me!"

December 1, 2016

Lex: "TJ, do you have a girlfriend?"
TJ: "Not anymore. I'm a wingman now for Jasiah and Conner."

~~~

I did not grow up in a home with boys. My family consisted of my mom, my sister, and me, and Lord knows my dad had a rough go of it being the only guy. I grew up playing with a bunch of boy cousins. From my experience with them, I knew that boys were free spirits and loads of fun. They had no boundaries in their thoughts and certainly didn't seem to exercise any restraints when it came to fun activities like playing football, racing, riding bikes, etc. They would tackle me just as hard as the next guy carrying the football and tease me unmercifully if I tried to wear makeup to school. I can recall many days of riding bikes with my cousins, climbing trees, and going to the lake to watch the alligators. We would ride for hours on our bikes all over the south side of St. Petersburg, Florida and I remember worrying about getting home before the streetlights came on or being chased by a dog at the next corner. They never seemed afraid when a dog would chase us, and now I know that it was because I was the slowest of the three of us. It was usually me, James, and Oscar. They were only a year or two older than me, and we spent a lot of years together as kids. They seemed to not care about boundaries, and I was totally crippled by them. They were carefree daredevils, and I was not. My cousins were always protective of me, but God knows they took no precautions when it came to sports. If I begged to play, I had to pay. I remember a family outing where I begged to play football with the boys. They didn't want a "girl" to play, but after the adults insisted, they taught me a lesson. One tackled me so hard I thought I saw stars floating around my head, and I remember thinking that I'd never ask if I could play football with them again. I will never understand how people recover after getting hit so hard in the game of football. Even after having these experiences, I never knew just how different boys were from girls until I had one girl and two boys of my own. After becoming a mother, the "B" word truly became a thing for me.

I spent most of my younger years following my cousins around but *living in a home with boys* was foreign to me. Having two boys of my own, I would quickly learn that there is nothing like the limitless mischief of a little boy with no boundaries. I can recall thinking "what in the world have I gotten myself into" the first time I walked into the bathroom to a puddle of pee on the floor, the first time I saw massive amounts of toothpaste left in the sink, or a collection of spider legs to be studied through TJ's microscope, and the garbage-riddled land fields they call their bedrooms! Are boundaries not built in? Why is it that the things they did never crossed my mind growing up? I don't know if girls are inherently better at knowing the boundaries than boys, but I would quickly find out. As soon as TJ and Lex were big enough to explore life, I knew that mine would be drastically different from anything I'd ever known. This was not the life I knew, and I had no idea of what was to come - especially all the talk that would be had about penises.

Penises are nothing to be ashamed of. They are synonymous to raising boys. Nevertheless, they are something we never talked about in my home growing up with girls, so I was mortified by how much we talked about them in a house of boys. During one of our visits to the Lowry Park Zoo in Tampa Florida, Lex, who was 5-years-old at the time, yells as loud as he can (he talks loud anyway), "Mommy, look at that Rhino's penis! It's so big! That's a big penis! Why won't he stop showing us?! Why won't he put it away?!" Oh my God, this went on for what felt like forever, but I'm sure it was only seconds. This totally topped the time the rhino farted at the zoo and both the boys walked around re-enacting the fart sounds of the rhino. Then there was the time TJ (5yrs old) asked me where I hid my penis. Boys are obsessed with their penises!

The boys would often take a shower with their dad when they were little. It kinda' put me in the mind of a boys' locker room, and it was always a great help and relief when that chore was done. During one of their locker room shower nights, Lex (5) asked me if I would be taking a shower with the guys to which I replied, "No."

Lex said, "Why? Too many penises?"

I said, "That's exactly why! I'm not in the penis club!"

Once TJ (who was 6 years old at the time), came home with a drawing from school. He pulled it out of his bag and gave it to me. There were 5 horses in the drawing, and each of them had these little hot dog looking things hanging from their tummies. I asked him what they were, and he said, "Mom, they are penises!" I asked, "So why do we have to see them?" He said, "'Cuz they don't have nowhere to put 'em (as if I were a was too simple to understand)!"

My boys taught me quickly that they were wild in the world. They were fearless and eager to explore life. I had just as much to learn as they did. How we set boundaries as parents and when we set them are crucial to the development of our teens. They are experiencing life for the first time through their rose-colored adolescent lenses, and boundaries are necessary for their core development. It is crucial that our teens learn to be responsible for their decisions and actions while controlling their attitudes and emotions. They should learn to be mindful of how their actions impact others and learn a healthy dose of humility and self-awareness.

Kelsie

I remember the day, a couple of years after Kelsie was born when I told all of my family and friends that I would never have any more children. I'd say it was because life would be too hard for them, having been through a divorce. I never thought I'd be married again, and no way was I having a baby without being married. I just did not want to raise another little one alone. Mostly I dreaded labor all over again. The pain of labor seemed like an experience close to death. I've often heard that you forget about the pain after the baby is born, **but that is a lie**. I remember all three births WITH the labor pains included. Twenty-two, eighteen, and sixteen hours of labor, and I remind them of it every time they act up.

Kelsie Mifflin (4)

Having my three kids was the best achievement I've ever accomplished. Kelsie was an absolute joy growing up, and she had the brightest personality. She had a way of making us all laugh constantly. She was the most beautiful baby I'd ever seen and had the brightest outlook on life as a little girl. I'll never forget one night when she was playing with her Barbie dolls, she looked at me and said "mommy the next time you go to the store will you get me a white Barbie doll? They are nice

Barbies, too." It was the sweetest and most innocent statement, and I had to laugh because as I gazed at her Barbies, they were indeed all brown. Naturally, as a mom with an African American daughter, I always bought dolls that looked like her. Already, she was teaching me to change.

TJ

TJ, my oldest son, could light up the world with his smile. He is a musician, athlete, model, and aspires to create prosthetics for limbless animals one day. At a young age he showed incredible athletic ability. We could tell this by observation. He would take off running and jump high into the air to land in a small, round clothes hamper. This scared the life out of me the first time he did it, but wow, was it amazing to watch! How do kids think up such things? He was always extremely fast and was built for sports and speed. He is a quiet and shy kid and has always enjoyed playing by himself. He was often the kid roaming away from the others while playing outside in search of animals, bugs, or reptiles. He was extremely curious about animals and bugs and when asked at a young age, "What do you want to be when you grow up?" he'd respond, "An animal doctor." As TJ got older, it was clear that he enjoyed outdoor activities also. Camping, hiking, fishing, and archery were all activities that he naturally gravitated to. TJ literally wants to spend every waking moment fishing and camping. The rest of the family, not so much. On occasion, I've taken him fishing, and Lord knows it is not my area of interest or expertise.

I remember one time I'd promised TJ for weeks that I'd take him fishing. However, I should have set up some boundaries for what he could expect on this outing. This was a parent fail, in my opinion. The day we agreed to go, TJ insisted that we leave very early in the morning. Apparently, that is the ideal time to catch fish. We cleared out my car and packed it with chairs, coolers, fishing rods, a tackle box, umbrellas, lunch boxes, and a cooler with prepared meat (TJ cut up fish chunks because he HAS to fish for catfish with a certain type of bait). We get to the lake, unpack all of the above items, trek to the fishing location of his choice, and set everything up. When TJ takes his first cast, the newly-purchased weight breaks off the rod and falls to the bottom of the lake. He looks at me and says, "I left the extra line and the other weight at the house."

We pack EVERYTHING up to go home to get his extra crap that should have been in the $&@/#%*#% tackle box from the start. We start ALL of the above over again only for TJ to cast his fishing rod a second time and lose the weight and line again.

Now the way my menopause is set up, it took everything in me not to lose it. There were too many things wrong in this situation: 1. I didn't want to go fishing to begin with, but TJ did, and that outweighed how I felt so yeah, I was not fully invested mentally. Plus, I'd promised that I'd take him, and I was not going to disappoint him. 2. I'm too old for this! Carrying all the equipment to and from the lake and setting it up was killing my back. It's a fact that many of us will suffer from degenerative disc disease by the time we are in our mid-fifties. Unfortunately, there's currently no cure for degenerative disc disease (DDD), and once you're diagnosed, it's typically a lifelong journey of learning to live with back pain, neck pain, or other symptoms. 3. I'd been bitten twice by something evil and he was circling me looking for another angle to attack for a third time. I WATCHED HIM DO IT! 4. What was in that useless tackle box? Why did I trust that TJ had done a better job of securing the second weight? It feels like I should have checked it before we left the house but what would I be looking for?

Needless to say, there were many other random rants that came to mind: I'm not going again unless there's a tricked out glamper...and are you kidding me - rain?!! Yeah, it's raining on us too. What are women my age, who were smart enough to have their kids in their twenties, doing right now? Clearly, I know nothing about fishing! If only I'd be ok with disappointing my kids. As I reflect on how miserable this experience was for me, my elder son got to go fishing, and he was happy and content just being in that space. All the way home he chattered incessantly. "I might catch a channel or a flathead catfish next time. I hope I can catch a 15-pounder. When Dad gets back, we are gonna' rent a boat and go fishing on the lake. You know if I hadn't lost my weight and would have sat out there longer, I might have caught a catfish 'cuz it's nothin' but a waiting game. Mom, did you know that there is an app that tells you a lot about fishing? It's called *Fish Brain*...and did you know that the best time to catch catfish is at night? That's when they are out feeding on Blue Gil and Shad. When we go fishing again (I was thinking "we???") I want to try a new lake the guy in Cabela's told me about. I think it's in Noblesville. When I catch some catfish will you help me clean them and cook them. I know cooking is not your best thing to do, but I'm sure if you call Grammie and Granddaddy they will tell you how to cook 'em."

Despite the mishaps, it became hard to care about my own discomfort when he was having so much fun. My learning in this situation was that I can't get frustrated with my family when I continue to overextend myself and don't set personal boundaries with them. I really need to do a better job of this.

In an effort to give TJ more adventurous opportunities, my husband would take him and Lex camping occasionally. T organized an annual Father & Son camping trip with several of the boys' friends' and their fathers. Moms were invited to come and stay overnight on the last night. I tried and failed every time. If squatting in the woods to pee and trying to sleep on the floor of a tent in a sleeping bag wasn't so unbelievably miserable for me, I might have stuck it out. Every time, I ended up leaving around 2:00 AM because the thought of a shower and the comfort of my own bed was too hard to shake. I blame it more on age and weight because when they were younger, I would at least stay until morning. Then there was the time when TJ had all four of us at the lake "herping." I remember asking him if it was a real word and could he spell it for me, so that I could look it up. Herping is the act of searching for amphibians or reptiles. How does a nine-year-old come across this kind of stuff? So, all four of us trekked over to the neighborhood lake that night with flashlights to help TJ search for frogs. I refuse to add snakes because THAT'S NOT WHAT I

AGREED TO HELP HIM FIND. Mostly I prayed that we would not come across snakes. By the end of the evening, I was the only one to spot a frog and honestly as crazy as this may sound, that was one of the best family moments ever. We had so much fun, and TJ was so happy. I will always be grateful that T and I did not say "no" to this lil' guy. His dream is to become a veterinarian one day and he can absolutely do it. I will admit that we have had to set some boundaries around the animals we will allow him to bring home because he has no filter for what's off-limits. He would bring home any critter he found if we would let him. Snakes and spiders are non-negotiables, and our lifestyle is too volatile to get a dog. He's been begging for one for a year, but we are hardly ever home. He currently owns two lizards and that is about all we can handle for now.

TJ has been playing the piano for ten years and recently started singing. He also spends several hours either at basketball practice, agility training, basketball training, or just at the court working on basketball fundamentals. Providing guard rails for him is extremely necessary as TJ is a perfectionist and will burn the candle at both ends. I'm always thinking of ways to get him to rest more and to give his knees a break.

Then there was the time TJ hid his trail cam in our bedroom across from our bed. T noticed it, and I could not believe it! TJ had gotten a trail cam one Christmas which he could leave outside overnight to record animals and observe their patterns. Thank God T and I had nothing of interest for him to see. I'm just too old for all this craziness and now I regret not recording something crazy on that lil' camera to get him back. We should have plotted to send him to military school or maybe boarding school somewhere. That would have been hilarious.

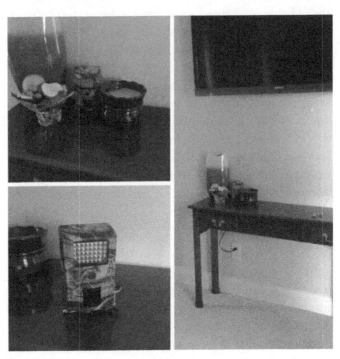

TJ's Trail Cam

Lex

Our younger son is an aspiring actor, writer, producer, and musician. Lex also loves sports and is an incredible athlete. He is extremely creative and has never been the type of kid to stay within boundaries. He never really liked coloring within the lines and had very little patience with constructive table time when he was little. He was always working on creative and dynamic ways to make us laugh, or to provoke us to think about things in a different way. I remember his third-grade teacher calling me one day to tell me about Lex at storytime. It was something she expressed that she'd never seen a kid do before and just wanted to share with me. Apparently, the class was given the chance to write their own stories to be read to the class at storytime. Lex's teacher said that the kids were starting to ask that Lex read his at the beginning of storytime because they were eager to hear what he had written. It turns out that Lex wrote a series of stories about a big baby who went on big adventures. I believe it was called "The Baby of Doom" and this baby would wreck some type of havoc on the town in each story. The twist was that Lex would use his classmates as the characters in the stories and his classmates absolutely loved it!

Lex started acting when he was 10 years old. Many of our friends and family would consistently say that Lex had a future in entertainment. T and I never really thought about it, but even in his pre-school, Jewel Christian Academy, Lex would always have the lead roles in plays. He was Adam in Adam and Eve, he was Jesus and fed the multitude, he was the Angel that came to the City of David to tell them to "fear not for a child is born," he even modeled in a Spring Fashion Show and ended up with a full-page picture in the Eastern Star monthly magazine. I remember the teacher telling me, "We never practiced him doing

"The Dougie" while walking down the runway. He's a mess." We both laughed because it was too comical.

At a very young age, Lex loved to make people laugh. T tells the story of one morning in the winter when he walked Lex to his classroom. T remembers Lex stopping him before they opened the door to go in to take his coat off, turn it around, and zip it closed backwards. When T asked him why, Lex said, "Because I like to make them yaaff (laugh)." Sure enough, when they walked into the room, Lex had his hoodie over his face and the kids broke into hysterical laughter! We both joked later that we were raising a "class clown."

Lex has always wanted to be an actor. I remember the day he asked me to put him in a commercial and a movie. My first response was, "You hate me, don't you? You're not involved in enough activities yet? I think y'all tryna kill me!" Lex fell out laughing and so did I. He was about six years old at the time, and I honestly didn't know how to help him with acting. Four years would pass before we took his request seriously. A good friend told us that there were summer classes at the Indianapolis Repertory Theatre and that we should enroll him. T signed both boys up for the IRT's four-week Summer Consortium. The boys had a blast. Four weeks into the school year we got an email inviting Lex to audition for the role of Stuart in the play *Stuart Little*. We were all excited that they thought enough of Lex to invite him to audition but we knew that there were other kids with previous acting experience and honestly it was all so new to us at the time that we were just happy for him to get the invite. Well, imagine our surprise when Lex got the part. Here is where it all began for him. Somehow, I believe that this was one of those magical moments where God was guiding us to be obedient, and we were. Little did we know (or foresee) the journey ahead. Even Lex's name was seemingly orchestrated for his future in acting. One night at the dinner table Lex (then Alex), at 5-years-old announced, "I want to be called Lex instead of Alex and from now on I not gonna' answer to Alex." And just like that "Alex" became Lex Lumpkin. We never asked why and in retrospect I wish I would have.

Lex completed his first year of acting with unbelievable ease. Once the ball started rolling, it was an amazing ride for all of us. Right after he completed Stuart Little at the IRT, a wonderful fellow thespian referred Lex to the Director of First Folio Productions and Lex auditioned for the role of Prince York in Shakespeare's Richard III. He got the part! His next opportunity would come just four short months later when he got the part of Dennis in five AT&T commercials with Peyton Manning, TY Hilton, and Demarco Murray. His next audition for the IRT was the part of Travis Younger in *A Raisin in the Sun*. During these two amazing years Lex would continue to get auditions through the talent agency, and that's when we were advised to give him an opportunity in LA.

Having a child in acting requires a huge investment of time and money including rehearsals just about every night, several shows a week, and spontaneous auditions that in most cases lead nowhere. With each performance and audition, either T, myself or my mom are there. Lex will never be left alone. I've learned that there is no limit at which parents will stop to help their children fulfill their dreams from sitting in the car for hours between shows to reading pages of scripts as the other characters in the scene as they practice. This journey to become an actor doesn't just involve hours of practice and preparation by Lex, but it also requires that the whole family makes some adjustments. We set boundaries for Lex because, while he does not show it, he is under tremendous pressure. We set them by protecting his time, making sure he gets "down time," and absolutely insisting that he demonstrates his commitment to acting by getting the necessary school requirements completed. In the midst of all the scene rehearsals, scripts that he has to memorize, corrective notes and line changes, he must also complete all of his school assignments, and pass his exams. He will not gain work permit approval if he does not make good grades in his classes. It is truly a testament to his commitment, dedication, fortitude, strength, endurance, and determination…I could go on and on but know that it requires that we all "dig deep." This requires a fine balance for T and I because both boys have their own paths to travel and we must keep both boys whole during this season of our lives.

Kids will test parents to find their boundaries. It would seem their only mission in life is to drive parents absolutely insane while coating their weapons with sugar. We love them like no other love we've ever known, and we want the absolute best for them. You'd be hard-pressed to find a parent who would disagree.

Every child deserves a parent who will be their biggest fan - a parent who cheers the loudest for them (literally), who will be brutally honest with them, a parent who will be patient with them, and a parent who will push them past their comfort zone. They deserve a parent who will stand tall for them and who will not make excuses for them, a parent who will make sacrifices for them and most of all a parent who will love the heck out of them with no conditions attached. This is what creates a kid who is destined to move mountains.

.

10.

The Hormones

September 12, 2016

Lex: "Mom, you and I are "shinny" people."
Me: In my head, "I don't feel so shinny."

March 20, 2018

Me on a snowy morning to Facebook: "Lex insisted on wearing shorts to school despite my reasoning with him to wear pants! Please join me in praying that he freezes his lil' a$$ off today and that the garage door key code malfunctions after school. Thanks in advance!"

~ ~ ~

It was a Friday afternoon when I barely made it home in time to meet the tutor for TJ's session. The previous Friday the tutor and I both had a talk with TJ about the usual "you must get all of your schoolwork done, you must turn it in on time, and log in incomplete assignments so that nothing falls through the cracks. He acknowledged that he understood and agreed to start doing it. This was my first clue that it would not get done. Puberty rarely agrees to do anything so responsibly and so readily. Yet, one week later, at the beginning of this Friday's session with the tutor, I had a bad feeling. The doorbell rang, and I opened the door for Ms. Shelly to enter. I called out for my son, and he was nowhere to be found. I called four times before he responded. Of course, by now, the tutor was sitting down ready to start the session. When he appeared, he was visibly irritated and had a head full of water and gel dripping down his face with a towel around his neck. How dare he have an attitude and why on earth was he doing his hair right now? His tutoring session is the same time every Friday. Why was he not ready? The tutor started asking TJ what happened with his math test since he currently had an incomplete for the grade. He began to talk, but the only words that came out of his mouth were "I don't know." This is a constant response of contention for me.

"What do you know? Why don't you ever know anything? Are you saying this with hopes that we will just go away and leave you alone?" These are the questions I ask myself internally. The second question from the tutor would be met with yet another answer from my son that was disjointed and made no sense.

"I don't know why I didn't log the work in my notebook." The third and final answer to the question sent me over the edge. I lost it. He hadn't logged any incomplete assignments in his workbook all week despite our previous discussions the week prior. I asked him if his goal in life was to be trifling.

"Do you think your assignments are just gonna' go away!" I yelled in front of his tutor and told him that he would be repeating the 8th grade and that we were calling that private school that he couldn't wait to go to in the fall to get our deposit back. As I looked him in his eyes, however, something happened...I can't say what it was because I simply don't know. All I knew was that a deep, dark sadness overwhelmed me. The summation of what I'd now come to realize was that TJ got a 30 on a homework assignment and his teacher changed it to a 50. Then TJ had a test in that same class on last Tuesday and, get this...turned it in incomplete and told his teacher that he would fill in the rest of the problems later...AND the teacher was willing to accept that. What in the entire hell is going on? Where the hell is that acceptable? *I don't think I had truly embraced the fact that TJ's 8th-grade teachers were enabling him by not demanding excellence from him.*

When a teacher cares they are invested in the painstaking time it takes to make sure their students are learning and understanding the work required to move to the next grade. Clearly, that was not the case in my son's current classroom experience. I've never in my life felt such hopelessness for my son, and it broke my heart. How must he be feeling about himself if his teacher doesn't have hope in him? These were emotions I'd never experienced before. I became extremely sad and ran to the basement because I didn't know what to do with all the misery rushing through me and had no way of knowing how to release it. As I dialed my husband, I had no control over my emotions. There was one other time that I cried like this about one of my kids, and it was years ago when Kelsie insisted that I let her go and live with her dad. I remember I cried every day for about a week. I couldn't imagine what two years of living in New York would be like for her. I didn't think that her dad would make the sacrifices that I was willing to make for her. I was wrong. He has been a great example for her, and she loves living in New York. She only had two more years of high school to complete at the time, but it was very hard telling her she could go. "There are only cornfields in Indiana," she said.

T answered my call, and by then I was crying hysterically and uncontrollably. I cried on the phone with him for what seemed like 20 minutes. I tried to wash my face, but my eyes were red, and my face was puffy and swollen. T didn't speak much, and I remember asking him if he could hear me as a way of checking to see if he was still there. He had never seen or heard me cry like this. I told him that I didn't think I was qualified to raise TJ to be the young man we both knew he could be. I told him that maybe I was too old for such a responsibility. I was afraid that TJ was not ready for young adulthood and that he could never be successful in high school at his current trajectory of maturity. I felt helpless and worried that I had failed yet another child.

I was also angry with TJ. How could he be so lazy, how could he not care at all about learning and making good grades? I thought he wanted to be a veterinarian. How could his teachers fail him by not demanding more from him in class, what was I doing to enable this behavior? I didn't cry, I *wailed!* He had no emotion when answering the questions, and I hurt for him - I felt *desperation* for his future. He was no longer a small kid and I knew that society views adolescent black boys as less innocent at the age of 10 as compared to their white counterparts. It is called *"adultification."* I had heard psychologist, Dr. Candice Norcott, talk about it on a documentary I had watched recently. I feared for TJ and cried harder as I prayed for God to touch him and protect him.

I returned upstairs and headed to the laundry room where the tears uncontrollably flowed again. I turned to leave, and there was Ms. Shelly, TJ's tutor. She grabbed me and hugged me. I didn't know that they could hear me. I was so embarrassed. She said sometimes we have to let them hit the bottom in order for them to understand. I knew what she was saying, but I feared that "the bottom" for my lil' black boy could be fatal. I thanked Ms. Shelly and apologized for my horrid display of emotions. Later, after she left, TJ apologized for making me cry. I thanked him, and we talked. I told him that I couldn't want more for him in life than he wanted for himself. I told him that no wife wants a lazy, trifling husband, no one wants to bring their pet to a veterinarian who doesn't know how to calculate milligrams to determine how much medication to give their dog, and no one wants to hear excuses about why you did not follow through on your responsibilities. I was down for the rest of that day. What would become of this smart and talented kid who seemingly had no interest in doing anything with his life? I had had a major meltdown, and it felt like someone close to me had died. Despite all of this, I knew that I could not let my hormones get the best of me and that I could not give up on him.

On any given day from the moment I open my eyes, I have about 200 thoughts simultaneously. "God, I'm fat, how did I let this happen again?...I should go downstairs and get on the elliptical, but I don't feel like it…. Where did all my energy go?" My eyes will sometimes water, but I fight back the tears because it won't provide a solution for me. Then I think, "I'm a fighter, I lost weight once before - even competed in a fitness competition - I can do it again...I don't want to get out of bed...there are so many things that need to get done! TJ has to get his braces tightened today but he really can't afford to miss any more school, and I totally forgot to take both boys to the dentist to get their teeth cleaned yesterday so I can't forget to reschedule that appointment. Oh my God, I have a lunch in service today! Did I order lunch? What did I talk to the doctor about last time? I gotta' remember to circle around to that conversation and don't forget that in our last national meeting we committed to asking bold questions, so which bold question do I need to ask?"

During this barrage of competing thoughts, I thumb through my phone to see which restaurant will deliver in the area of the territory I will be in today. I also get sidetracked by Facebook's ability to make me happy and content. These days I'm a total addict to the "feel-good" factor. Side note here: Your brain releases dopamine when you feel pleasure—while eating your favorite foods, for example, or during sex. The "feel-good" factor, however, is one of the elements behind dopamine's darker side. Several illegal recreational drugs stimulate its release and increase the amount of dopamine in the brain. The increased feelings of pleasure that result from these drugs make users susceptible to addiction. Dopamine relieves stress and stress provokes the need for more dopamine. It's a vicious cycle which is exploited by the most "innocent" of culprits - coffee, sex, chocolate, shopping, crafting, social media, and alcohol.

"Dopamine release is also responsible for people becoming addicted, in that [people] are always seeking pleasure, so that they can reach higher and higher dopamine levels," explains Harald Sitte, of MedUni Vienna's Institute of Pharmacology, speaking on the occasion of the September 2016 Dopamine Conference at Vienna University. "Dopamine is the reason why a lot of people are constantly seeking to satisfy their cravings," Professor Sitte confirms[viii]. I make this statement to raise awareness to the fact that we are not in a good place when we are always looking for a dopamine high. Surprisingly, both menopausal and pubescent people are susceptible to high levels of stress and, therefore, to some form of dopamine addiction. Kiddos under stress and mamas under stress, both seeking relief from stress, make a dangerous combination. For example, puberty might get addicted to Fortnite to escape the stress caused by menopause's constant nagging. Menopause will, in response, get lost in social media or crafting, take her eye off the ball, and lose sight of what's really going on with puberty (resulting in puberty doing whatever they want and menopause nagging more, and puberty seeking more stress relief). Unfortunately, puberty won't just get addicted to video games, and menopause won't just get addicted to social media. There are much more nefarious addictions out there which tear families apart every day. Learn to recognize when an "occasional" stress reliever becomes a constant need like when an evening glass of wine becomes 2 or 3 or 4. When this happens, it's time to quit and seek help not just for the addiction, but also for the true source of the stress. Similarly, when puberty is playing 2, 3, or 4 hours of video games per day - or worse - consuming pornography, drugs, or alcohol, stop and consider what's really going on. Their developing brains are highly susceptible to damage and addiction. They will need your help and your prayers to steady the ship.

I digress, as I'm looking through Facebook and Instagram and several web searches to validate something that caught my attention. I'm immediately reminded that I must still order lunch. Then there is the haunting thought that the boys haven't been practicing as much as they should for an upcoming piano concert and then I'm sad again because there doesn't seem to be enough time in the day to get it all done. There are clean clothes all over my bedroom floor that need to be separated and put away, crap is scattered all over my house, and something sticky was spilled on the kitchen floor, and no one bothered to clean it up. Instead they left it for me just so my foot can get sticky as well. Not to mention that I need to get to the grocery store, there are still Christmas decorations laying around the house to be hung, and I have purchased exactly zero gifts! Cards must be written out for the boys' teachers, piano instructor, tutor, and bus driver. Oh, and I need to get by the pharmacy, and the pet store to pick up crickets and a light for TJ's lizards, and oh yeah - TJ needs earbuds for school. I also need to mail a birthday card to Kumi, my grandson (I'm so glad he's still too little to know how late it is). Did I take my synthroid today? Oh, and don't forget that Lex's self-taped audition is due by 9:00 AM tomorrow morning. A venti Starbucks Mango Dragonfruit tea with lemonade and a load of sugar would be delicious right now...definitely gotta' get one. What time is it? Did the boys miss the bus? Are they arguing this early in the morning? I can't handle this! What is that awful smell? OMG, did my son dump the entire bottle of cologne over his head this morning? In the midst of this, I'm moved to spontaneous prayer, *"Thank you Lord for blessing our family. Forgive me for my constant complaints and help me to become the person you would have me be. Help me to control my raging hormones, Lord, and not be mad at my kids and husband all of the time. Sigh. What am I gonna wear today? Nothing fits anymore, and I refuse to buy larger clothes! God, I'm fat! Amen."*

I could never have prepared for the mood swings, irrational behavior, aches and pains, and the inability to sneeze without a bit of pee escaping my control that accompany this phase of life. Not to mention that any monotonous noise will drive me absolutely out of my mind and any and everything is too much stimulation. I swear if my son says "mom" one more time I'm gonna strap on a Depends, get in my car and drive west until I reach the ocean - and I mean it this time!

Many women plan their pregnancies. I, however, did not. When I got married a second time, we both agreed that we'd have two kids and I'd get my tubes tied. This was my idea given that I'm 11 years older than my husband and had already had a daughter from my first marriage. I was done after TJ and Lex. I never really thought about menopause and puberty living together in a hotbed of volatility one day. Imagine placing a small rock in a blazing fire. A rock in these conditions will pop as it heats. Most of the time I feel like I'm that small rock. I really should have considered the implications of the two most drastic hormones coupled with the most major changes in one's life trying to make a go of it together. But alas, we are thriving and surviving, and it's working. Yes, we are bound to their success. As an older parent, I made the choice to have kids later in life and I must embrace all that comes with it. I love my boys and like most parents want the very best that life can offer them.

Despite my overwhelming feelings of exhaustion, I will not let them down. I will go to a million basketball games on Sunday evenings cheering the loudest (true story). I will go to Walmart at 2:00 AM to film whatever my son needs for a project he's working on, and I will get up at 5:00 AM every Friday to take my son to his tutor if that's what is required for him to succeed - whether I want to or not.

‹ December   ☰   🔍   +

S	M	T	W	T	F	S
9	10	11	12	13	14	15

Sunday December 9, 2018

all-day	Christmas at the Zoo

2 PM

Team Stephens vs. Chargers Orange
Best Choice Fieldhouse - Court ORG

3 PM

Chargers Blue vs. Indy Hoops 8th White
Best Choice Fieldhouse - Court ORG

4 PM

5 PM

Chargers Blue vs. Indy Hoops 8th Orange
Best Choice Fieldhouse - Court ORG

6 PM

7 PM

Circle City Racers vs. Indy Nets 2024 Gray
Best Choice Fieldhouse - Court YEL

8 PM

9 PM

Today   Calendars   Inbox

MENOPAUSAL PARENTS LIVING WITH PUBERTY:

-Love trap music.

-Know slang totally against their will.

-Don't mince words. Calls a penis a penis, and a vagina a vagina.

- Embarrass their kids with many forms of candor - not to be mean but just because life has taken on new meaning at 50 years old.

-Will parent other people's pubescent kids as if they were their own.

- Will have a mortified reaction to watching their kids play Fortnite as it makes no sense whatsoever! A sword is actually stuck through a plunger and used to knock down walls. Listen: "Brain matter cannot be grown back!"

-Communicate with their teens through text messaging. (I learned this from my girlfriend and Sorority Sister, Renee Blake.)

- Know text codes, text language, and snap streaking (modern Day shorthand) Side note: parents sign up for Talking Tech!

- Use a lot of humor and wine to keep from dropping puberty off at the nearest safe haven shelter, driving off, and never looking back.

- Are continuously reminded of just how much older they are than their kids' friends' parents with questions like, "Mike's mom plays videos games. Are you just too old to play? Maybe you don't like video games 'cuz they weren't around when you were a little girl." Me in my head: "WTH?! Don't they know I have feelings? Video games are the bane of my existence."

- Are constantly reminded of how old they are in general: "Will your teeth start falling out soon? Whoa, that will be cool! Will you be able to take your teeth out like Grammie? Did Jesus drive a horse or a car back when you were a little girl? I want a baby sister, are you too old to have more babies? I just can't believe that you didn't have video games when you were a kid. Wow! Like what did you do all day for fun? I can't wait till I'm 54 so I can do whatever I want like you!"
- Get Barbie dolls for Christmas (really sweet gift).
- Watch their kids get hyped up "hitten dem folk" while using grunts like "Aaaaye, aiight, whaaa, ya …[ix]"

-Watch their younger husband learn something new on Clash Royale from puberty. Lol!

11.

T'Lisa-isms

If you're a busy momma like me and want to speed-read this book to get the highlights - this section is for you!

Raising kids is the best and hardest thing I've ever done. No one ever knows the depth of utter joy, love, compassion, mental misery, frustration, and shame we sometimes deal with as parents. Kids have a way of bringing out every emotion known to man. Still, we press on. It's like pushing a large boulder up a never-ending mountain, but the "rest stops" overlooking the vast landscape of their growth and accomplishments are well worth the pain of pushing them.

Remedy for "I can't": I make the boys recite this every time they'd say, "I can't." "There is nothing in the world that I cannot do with the help of Jesus."

Something miraculous happened. They stopped saying "I can't" and started believing they could.

The pain of honesty is measured by your efforts. Low effort = Painful Honesty. High Effort = Honesty you want to hear.

Teach your kids at an early age (preferably when they start talking) to say, "I'd be happy to."
Example:
Mom: "Go back upstairs and brush your teeth."
Son/daughter: "I'd be happy to."

Go hard and dream big! No one is stopping you!

Your best opportunity for change is right now. Time won't wait for you.

The beauty of children radiates as a result of awesome parents! There is a special magic in it.

Love them hard and forgive them harder.

Fake it till you make it! Of course, I didn't make this one up, but I tell my kids this constantly. Always work on building their confidence. I also tell them to remember that people don't know what you don't know until you tell them.

Shape a person's perception of you. Don't leave it to them to decide. You never know when you might come up in conversation so give them the words you want to be repeated about you. Never leave your story to someone else to tell. You are who you decide you will be.

Attitudes truly are contagious. So, ask yourself one question, is mine worth catching?

There is healing in spiritual truths. Be honest with yourself first.

It's all about controlling your thoughts. When we are weak, we have no control. When we are strong, we can conquer all!

Stay strong and keep grinding with a purpose and it's yours!

The truth is like water trapped in the crevice of a rock. It will always find its way out.

Let people come to their own conclusions about who you are…just influence and guide their decisions positively!

Your spouse and kids need space to be who they are and not who you want them to be.

List your parent defaults and strive to change them. For example, yelling, "No, what the hell did I say?" is my fail of choice. A "parent default" is basically a "parent fail" moment. When you have a knee jerk reaction to a negative behavior or answer when you become frustrated with your kids, you are susceptible to a parent fail. It can happen when you are rushing out the door running late, when you've lost your patience and have reached the boiling point, etc.)

In life, when you get "GOOD" advice, follow it to the letter!

Advice can come from people of all ages, even children.

I tell the boys to embrace their haters. You need haters in your life because they drive you to be better than you ever thought you could be.

Just because you are not afraid to say it, doesn't mean you should.

Live on the bright side of it all!

Your attitude will be one of the most useful tools in your toolbox.

Make sure that your expectations are realistic.

Which will you choose? To soar with the eagles or gobble with the turkeys. Just know that your decision will influence your investment.

I can't care more than you do.

Borrow someone's kids if you don't have your own, they are priceless, and you need them in your life.

It's easy to be a bad parent and hard to be a good parent. You have to put in the work to raise solid citizens!

My hardest job in life is not to impose my fears and jaded views on my boys. Let them live in their innocence for as long as possible!

Imagine if all the kind and loving people in the world could hold hands to form one large human circle around all the mean and hateful people and literally love the hell out of them. THAT would be awesome!

Life is like the earth's vegetation reclaiming the land. Roots break through concrete to bask in the sun, trees grow up and out of hollow steel posts, and vines creep along structured walls asserting their presence. So is the same in life. Life has no boundaries or rules. It's going to do what it does despite mankind!

If you don't like what you see when you look at yourself in the mirror... CHANGE!!!! Stop trying to transfer your ugliness on to others!

I despise and am intolerant of people who think they are "entitled."

Sometimes it's YOU and not your kid. Look in a mirror!

Don't be in denial! Puberty wants to confuse, consume, and control you.

We ALL think our children are GREAT and THEY ALL ARE! Not just yours!!!

Set your expectations of certain family members appropriately to avoid a broken heart and broken kids at all cost.

Find your kid's superpower and work like hell to make them believe in it.

Be the parent/person you'd like to see your child become.

If you break wind let the good folks around you know (say, "excuse me") so they have a way out!!! Please don't pretend it didn't happen!

Always find something positive to tell your kid. They thrive on the satisfaction and approval of their parents.

Please, for the love of God and all that is Holy....do not make excuses!!!! Just say it, "I forgot...I was late because I'm trifling...or I didn't show up because I didn't want to come!"

Your "core values" are exposed to everyone you meet. Please don't think you are hiding.

Be who you are and don't apologize! Side note: If you are an ass you will get ignored...your apologies fall on deaf ears. Don't be an ass!

Kids should always "right" their wrongs - (so should adults) they should apologize to the teachers for disrupting class (if they get into trouble) and apologize to their peers when they disagree (if they are in the wrong).

No adult wants to raise another adult! Get it together!

I use the expression, "REALLY!?" quite often and realized that what I'm really saying is "What the fuck? Who knew?"

So random, but one of my favorites: Train that abdominal wall...always hold your stomach in[x].

When you begin to modify your life in a way that is uncharacteristically you, or in a way that is not organic to who you've grown to know, it's time to take a long hard look at your life and what is happening to you and around you.

Prepare yourself for any and everything that comes your way when two families are joined together in marriage. Lord, it is true that you marry the whole family and all the personalities that come with it. Unfortunately, some family members will try to force their will on you or try to control you. I love being a team player, but not the victim of "Jedi Mind Tricks." Don't ever be afraid to push back on people when their leaning in on you is inconsiderate and intended to take from you. This is especially true of family.

Money isn't everything.

When people give you "shade"...EITHER enjoy the protection from the elements they are blocking you from OR you probably did something fucked up...so check yourself.

Sex is important.

Licking a person is not ok!

Be who you are and don't apologize! Side note: If you are an ass, you get ignored...your apologies fall on deaf ears.

Don't kiss new babies on the mouth, face or hands - their mommas should not have to check you on this.

Stay outta' your son/daughter's marital affairs unless absolutely non-negotiable things happen.

Stay all over and in between puberty's business, 'cuz any underaged business of theirs becomes business of yours.

Clear BS out of your life immediately. This includes trifling family members.

Don't put sugar on shit and tell me it's candy.

Learn how to hear what's not being said.

I have decided that I will no longer be embarrassed or apologize for investing all that I have in our kids. My husband and I spend most of our time, energy, and money on our boys' futures.

Practice saying, "absolutely not!" it may come in handy from time to time. Learn to say "absolutely not" when you have too many plates spinning. Those two words could very well save your life one day. That's a phrase I picked up from a dear friend and it lets people know when they've crossed the line.

Love them through all the emotion (yours and theirs) and trying times. You are the adult and the parent.

Don't let your hormones turn you into the nagging parent they dread to see. Listen more and talk less. Empower them to make decisions that affect their daily lives but stay close enough to them to help them navigate the rocky path. Say, "I trust that you will make the right decision."

Try not to give in to your dreaded menopausal emotions. It can lead you down a path of negative interaction with your teen. Counting to ten and blowing out air slowly tends to help me gather my thoughts before I speak. ... or not.

Our teens are not our friends, but their interests should be of interest to us.

Learn one or two things about what they love the most.

Don't take yourself so seriously that you forget to laugh with them.

Their hard day at school should mean enough to us to stop and listen.

Teens should always be seen AND heard.

Menopause is no excuse to ruin your teen's day.

Find ways to connect with your teen that you've never tried before. If they like video game stores, deliberately drive to that type of store and ask them to show you their favorite games.

Yes, they are messy. They will not clean their rooms, they will leave garbage on the counter located closest to the garbage can, they will not take their clothes to the laundry room, they will eat all of your food, they will stay up texting their friends, they will leave toothpaste in the sink, they will have an attitude despite what we say because they are still growing and developing mentally.

Teens will most often not have the answer to the question, "Why?"

Teens will mumble most of their teen years (about seven years).

I have to remind myself that with each stage of my kids' development, it is a stage that they have never journeyed before, therefore every developmental corner they turn, they will need help to navigate it.

You will not know your teen's best ability when you are always focusing on their deficiency.

If you feel like you are always fussing, you are! Stop it!

You must have a positive vision of their future in order to lead them to it.

When your teen has shown passion in a certain area, champion their interests, and push them far beyond their capabilities. Look for a master mentor in that area and find creative ways to push them more.

When menopause and puberty compete at a game of Fortnite the world is a happier place.

Please learn your teen's text abbreviations and slang language.

Be present in their lives.

Never tolerate disrespect.

My two sons are polar opposites! They both require different parenting skills from me, and I'm exhausted and unequipped! As a parent, I often feel inadequate because I DON'T KNOW THE ANSWERS! I'm literally "building this plane in flight" (stole that saying from work). The worst is that sometimes I'm too tired to look for parts to build the plane. Parenting is not for the faint of heart. It took me 28 years to learn this, and the learning continues.

I was not always as open-minded with raising my kids as I am now. In the past, I've broad-brushed my ideas and opinions onto my kids because it was easy and required little effort. My (now adult) daughter Kelsie, was raised in a single-parent home and I was young and clueless. (Forgive me, Kel!) I, for the longest, tried to push my "way" and my "agenda" on her. I have learned a lot since those years.

Young people are the absolute better versions of us! They come packaged with a whole host of great things that we have never seen before. Let them try sports, music, gymnastics, dance, explore nature, color their hair, etc. and get out of their way! Our job is to set them up for success!

Always speak life into their dreams. Be their biggest fans! I firmly believe that our children become who we tell them they are. So, years ago when the boys were very young (at the age of a million questions) I'd say things like, "You can't blend in when you were born to stand out," or "You were destined for greatness," or "You will soar with the eagles and not gobble with the turkeys." I'd then say to them, "Why?" and I'd answer for them, "Because eagles fly, and turkeys get eaten!" "WHICH ONE WILL YOU BE?"

I don't know who my children will be when they

become adults, but I pray that they are great contributors to society. We hope that we've taught them to make good decisions and to be strong enough to push past the obstacles they will face in life.

They must make mistakes in order to learn! Tell them firmly when they are wrong and teach them ALWAYS to make it right. This is an absolute must in our home! I love it when they can learn from a really bad situation. My boys get caught being 12 and 13 quite often. Lol! We teach them, "Mistakes will happen in life, but that's not the big deal. The big deal is all in how you make it right! Now how are you going to make this right?"

Build an environment for them to learn and explore. When we put limits on playing video games, they were never at a loss for other things to do (vs the "I'm bored" syndrome). They could play the piano, read, play board games, bake a cake, work on one of their short stories, make a movie, compose a song, write a play, shoot pool, ride their bikes, watch a movie, invent something, etc. There are many things they can do besides video games.

My kids drive me crazy at times, but I have successfully adjusted my expectations! They need space to be who they are and not who I want them to be. I try hard to get out of their way and see what happens.

TOMMALISA LUMPKIN

MENOPAUSE VS. PUBERTY

12.

Epilogue

(Parting thoughts. They grow up fast.)

I am learning to navigate the terrain of my boys' tumultuous teen years gently. These teenagers will test our very will to feed them. I can't tell you the number of times I've lost it with my boys. From morning to midnight, it can sometimes be a constant battle for me. Waking up to cap-less toothpaste and mouthwash to the empty cereal box laying on the island right above the garbage, I work hard to contain my nerves.

Despite the debilitating urge to be left alone, you will find that your pubescent kid is still in a state of dependency and development. They will continue to need our guidance as they move into adulthood and as much as we look to the golden age of "18" to be liberated from them, there are many studies to prove that their brains are not fully developed until way past the age of 25. So be the guiding light of reason and love them through their high school years despite themselves. Try very hard not to yell so much and give them room to figure out who they are. Gently guide them in the right direction with love and understanding despite your desire to clobber them multiple times. Try not to be so predictable in your responses. Check your parent defaults and think about the situation before you respond quickly with a "no." I've fallen in that rabbit hole only to realize that it could possibly have been a yes or maybe. I should have listened longer and asked a few more questions. Don't continue to repeat yourself over and over again.

Life is too short to dwell on all the wrongs of our teens. They will make mistakes, they will trip over themselves, they will test the limits of every boundary we've ever set for them. To impose our will and to constantly try to figure out what we did or where we went wrong will not yield the answers we seek. I have lived long enough to know that parents aren't perfect and while I used to think that I had it all figured out, I now know that I don't.

It's hard to navigate the halls of emotions and physical change that plague women during menopause. The benefits of wisdom, life experience, and maturity make us the resident experts on how to live happily with teenagers in our midst. Be strong parents and remember that they will soon be gone, starting their own families and living their own lives. Invest the time NOW and be proud of the work you've done.

Inspiration for the Book Cover

TJ (10), Me (50), Lex (9) - September 26, 2015

These two tried to drive me crazy while at dinner with Mom, Dad, and T. I was tickled, tricked, used as a cot, heckled and I'm pretty sure I ate something that was not originally on my plate. Will I REALLY miss them when they leave for college?

Let's Stay in Touch

I'd love to hear about your MVP journey! Follow me on Instagram (@tommalisalumpkin) and Facebook (@tommalisalumpkin) for a continual stream of updates and outbursts!

Endnotes

_____

i https://developingchild.harvard.edu/resources/what-is-executive-function-and-how-does-it-relate-to-child-development/
ii https://developingchild.harvard.edu/resources/what-is-executive-function-and-how-does-it-relate-to-child-development/
iiihttps://www.thescienceofpsychotherapy.com/prefrontal-cortex/u
iv https://developingchild.harvard.edu/resources/what-is-executive-function-and-how-does-it-relate-to-child-development/
v   v

https://www.nimh.nih.gov/health/publications/children-and-mental-health/index.shtml.

vihttps://www.google.com/amp/s/www.cosmopolitan.com/politics/news/amp31528/14-misconceptions-about-domestic-violence/
vii https://www.healthyplace.com/abuse/adult-physical-abuse/women-abuse-why-some-men-abuse-women
viii (University Health News - https://universityhealthnews.com/daily/depression/what-is-dopamine-understanding-the-feel-good-hormone/)
ix https://youtu.be/yVYE88RMd4E

xx http://en.m.wikipedia.org/wiki/Core_(anatomy)

Made in the USA
Las Vegas, NV
18 September 2021